SHIPWRECK INVESTIGATED,

FOR THE CAUSE

Of the great loss of lives with which it is frequently attended;

AND

A REMEDY PROVIDED,

IN A PORTABLE AND PRACTICABLE

LIFE PRESERVING APPARATUS;

Which is calculated for, and is necessary to become, a part
of every ship's equipment.

Its Efficacy is also Proved,

By demonstrative application to the cases of a great number of recent
Shipwrecks herein narrated; from which it is evident, that at
eight of them only, it might have been rendered
instrumental in preserving

NEAR TWO THOUSAND LIVES.

A great number of the narratives of Shipwrecks are very interesting,
and many of them have never been before published.

By HENRY TRENGROUSE,

HELSTON.

"The end and the means are always joined together in the
purposes and decrees of God.   But as the care of the end belongs to
God, so the care of the means belongs to us, and must be used when
they may, and where they can be used."

BURKITT ON ST. PAUL'S SHIPWRECK.

𝔉𝔞𝔩𝔪𝔬𝔲𝔱𝔥:

Printed and Published by James Trathan.

SOLD BY BALDWIN, CRADOCK, AND JOY, LONDON; AND
ALL OTHER BOOKSELLERS.

1817.

PREFACE.

WHEN I first began to write, I intended only an introduction to a description of an Apparatus I have invented, for the preservation of lives and property, in case of Shipwreck; but was insensibly led much farther into the subject, than I had even thought on. I then decided on the propriety of collecting my ideas and conclusions, and of committing them pretty largely to print, as the most eligible and efficacious method of diffusing the convictions which possessed my mind; and of conveying them to those, who, from their circumstances and situations in life, are the most likely to feel themselves more particularly called upon, to promote the adoption of my plan.

Notwithstanding having thus decided, I am fully sensible of my own inferiority to do justice to the subject with my pen; and because I do not consider myself qualified for a public writer, and am also apprehensive, lest my manner of expression may not be such as to engage, I respectfully solicit patient attention: and, (however exalted your station in life) IN THE NAME OF HUMANITY, beg a dispassionate and serious perusal of this little pamphlet. This I flatter myself will be afforded, from a persuasion that (in the estimation of every person possessed of humane and christian feelings) the defectiveness of composition, will be amply overbalanced by the importance of the subject; the serious attention of the humane and sympathetic only, do I expect to arrest; and I fondly hope, in this enlightened age, the numbers will not be few.

If maritime history is examined, it will be found to contain most distressing accounts of shipwrecks, attended with loss of human lives in melancholy numbers. And it would appear, that the destruction of the thousands, and the tens of thousands that have become victims to this insatiate devouring enemy, has been assented to, and narrated as, a necessary part of shipwreck itself:—that the loss of lives must follow as matter of course—unavoidably so. On this ground may be presumed a reason, why an investigation of shipwreck and its direful consequences, has never taken place :—a reason why shipwreck has never been scrutinized, with a view to discover why and how it is so fertile in destruction of human life: and consequent upon this follows one strong reason, why the means which have been introduced as life-preserving means, have proved so very ineffective. Considering however, that effects cannot be possibly counteracted, without first ascertaining the cause that produces them, (while contriving my life-preserving apparatus,) I have employed my feeble talents to investigate shipwreck; not with a view to discover the reason why any persons are by it destroyed, but to discover the cause of such excessive numbers becoming its victims: that by such discovery, I might be enabled to apply the Remedy with all possible effect.

By perusing the narratives of shipwrecks,—and by reflecting on those I have myself witnessed,—I readily discover that vast numbers are destroyed, NOT by wreck itself;—but by its Frowns! In many instances, the greater part of those destroyed IN wreck, are not destroyed BY wreck;—but by the auxiliary destroyers to which shipwreck gives abundant birth. I may say that Fear is the first born offspring ; and after it follows Anxiety, Perturbation, Distress, Anguish, Agony, Despair, Demagement, with every evil upon the mind, that the love of life, and the dread of losing it, can possibly produce :—operating in various ways, as the minds of various persons may be predisposed to receive impressions and impulsions; but with equal certainty to insure the ruin of all ; either by disarming them of the power to make exertions, or else by urging them precipitately into the use of means, that are in themselves destructive. In this latter way, destruction is more generally prevalent, in proportion as the wreck may be near the shore.

I might bring forward a variety of instances to prove the dreadful operating of shipwreck upon the minds of poor sufferers ; but beg particular attention to the narratives of the loss of the Grosvenor, and the Vryheid Indiamen; Droits De L' Homme, Namur, Raven, and Wager, men of war. In the narrative of Captain Campbell's Shipwreck it is said; "the unfortunate, english purser who was drowned, had not courage sufficient to make an effort to save himself, notwithstanding he was a man of known courage·" But there is also a vast number of instances, wherein the poor sufferers could not assist themselves, "even were their minds composure itself: because they had no means." I mention the Amicus, Boadicea, Blue Bonnet, Horatio, John and Agnes, Litchfield, Leonora, Phæton, Sceptre, San Juan, Invincible, &c. From whatever cause our fellow creatures are suffering, they have a claim upon our sympathy—from whatever cause they are perishing, they have a claim upon our help.

If shipwreck is traced back to the earliest period of modern history, it is discoverable that it produced then, effects and consequences similar to what it does now; and that whatever changes may be produced, in other respects, by the revolution of time, it appears that the love of life has suffered no variation; that it has ever reigned predominant, and that it is now the same as it ever has been. I am not aware that the account of any wreck is correctly handed down to us from so early a period as that of St. Paul. In the 27th chap. of the Acts, it is very circumstantially described; and throughout, bears perfect resemblance to shipwreck of the present day. Burkitt, in his commentary says, "Observe the hopeless, helpless, comfortless state which they are now reduced to. Through consternation of mind and horror of death, they had made no set meal for fourteen days; they had eat so little, it might be called a continual fasting." Now, as in the cases I have called particular attention to, so here, it was the love of life, and the dread of not being able to preserve it that produced all the evil upon their minds; for in the 20th verse it reads, "all hope that we should be saved was taken away." And it was only by the repeated and animating exhortations of St. Paul, with assurances of their lives being preserved, that the sailors were prevailed upon to take nourishment, and "to be of good cheer;" and finally to return to their duty, and to use those exertions which were likely to promote preservation; and on which indeed it solely depended. The reader will have the goodness to compare this shipwreck with those of recent date.

The narratives of shipwrecks appendant on the Investigation, will be found very interesting in themselves; especially by those who have not already had an opportunity of reading them: but their particular intention is to afford proofs of the excessive numbers of lives that fall sacrifices to shipwreck—to afford proofs of the more immediate and particular cause—and to afford proofs how my Apparatus may be applied, and rendered a general remedy. In fine, as the narratives have afforded me much matter to elucidate the subject—their being annexed is particularly intended for the reference of readers; that they may be thereby empowered to compare and judge for themselves; and that they may behold the evidences therein contained, which so clearly corroborate what I have advanced.

The Apparatus that I have after nearly ten years' application (not constant) been enabled to contrive, may be used for a variety of valuable purposes in maritime concerns; and for such purposes, as I am certain, have never before been thought on. Its originally intended, and most important use, is to preserve lives; but its powers may be extended to the preservation of much property, and may be rendered instrumental (in certain cases) even to preserve ships!

Being well convinced by Experience (as well as by Reason) that to render any contrivance for saving lives in case of wreck, extensively or generally useful, it must be such as to admit of being kept on shipboard; I have studied much for portability and simplicity; in which I have so well succeeded, as for its magnitude to be accommodated to a pilot boat; and its use (either by day or by night) to the most common capacity.

To afford assistance (when stress of weather renders it necessary) the opening a communication with a rope, is the first thing to be effected; and which to do with promptitude and precision, is of the utmost importance. I therefore feel great satisfaction in reflecting on the success that has at last attended my labours in devising the means to do this; my methods being such as induce me to believe they are so superior, as not to be equalled by any thing which is not on the same principle! I have not tried how far I can project a line, but I have no doubt of being able to do it with all necessary precision, upwards of half a mile. With the other parts of the Apparatus, I am also fully satisfied; as to their simplicity and portability, are combined accommodation and security, and may be used with the most possible rapidity. Upon the whole, I think I have good reason for, and do feel disposed, to congratulate the whole world generally; but those who traverse the wide ocean, and their friends particularly, on having been enabled by the assistance of Divine Providence, to produce an Apparatus that promises to be so extensively beneficial: and the more so, as it is altogether such, as not to require winters to pass, shipwrecks to occur, and lives to be put in jeopardy, for its capability to be ascertained by actual service; for every thing belonging to it is so plain, as to be readily comprehended by inspection: and I fondly flatter myself that all who afford it due consideration, will be possessed of a conviction similar to myself.

Having expressed my belief, that the importance of the subject will induce the humane to give a serious perusal; so now I express my hopes that on perusal, the evidences in favour of my life-preserving plan, will appear so plain, and I trust prove so stimulative, as to engage their interest in forwarding the adoption of it. Of myself, I cannot bring it into practice; I therefore in the name of HUMANITY solicit the necessary aid; being well assured that the blessings of thousands will flow from the fruits of its utility, as grateful acknowledgments for having their days prolonged. And when it is considered that very many in the time of shipwreck, betake themselves to excessive use of spirits, and (with others) fill their mouths with horrid imprecations, and in such a state are hurried from time into eternity:—will not their fate appear doubly distressing? And will not their preservation become additionally interesting and desirable?

I beg also respectfully to ask, may not preserving the lives of such poor creatures from premature death, lead to the preservation of their never dying souls? In the name of HUMANITY, do I again solicit patronage for what promises such very extensive good. As an individual, I humbly confess that I feel a most lively and anxious concern, that my plan may be reduced to immediate practice. And well I may, when I have such confidence in its efficacy; and calculate (from the strongest,—the most unequivocal evidences, as the cases themselves supply) that the Apparatus at the wrecks of eight only of those herein narrated, might have been rendered instrumental to have preserved, NEAR TWO THOUSAND fellow creatures!!

Helston, August 12, 1817.

SHIPWRECK

INVESTIGATED, &c.

WHEN the mind seriously reflects on the vast number of Shipwrecks that happen every year, and on the calamities, and extensive destruction of human life that attend them, it cannot but feel appalled.

To attempt description of the horrors and distresses which follow in the train of Shipwreck, would be useless; because they cannot be fully conceived but by those only, who are so unfortunate as to be its victims. However, it may readily be conceived to be big with terror and woe, even in its mildest form : and surely the calamities attending the many wrecks that have recently happened, (and several of them on our own shores) are sufficient to arouse even the most lithargic, to compaisssion and sympathy.

There cannot be any doubt entertained that Sailors of all nations (generally speaking,) use every effort they are capable of making, to effect preservation when surrounded with danger. And I am ready to believe, that those of our own nation are adequate to any thing that seamanship or courage can perform : but *they* cannot overcome *impossibilities* any more than others, nor produce effects, but such as are in unison with their causes.

B

Believing thus of sailors, it is presumed that when they are upon a *lee shore*, they do not suffer their vessel to be stranded without first striving to *work off;* or trying the efficacy of their anchors and cables. In either case, if it is not dark, or thick fog, they have an opportunity of surveying the coast; and of selecting a spot the most favourable in appearance, on which to run their vessel, (if going ashore cannot be prevented,) to secure the preservation of their lives, and as much as possible of the property which is entrusted to their care. This is a prudent measure, and is generally the last they adopt, or indeed have to adopt; for with the loss of anchors and cables, it may be said, that their resources are expended, either towards effecting the preservation of their vessel or themselves. In such a situation, all they can do is to hoist a sail or two, & bear away for their chosen spot; wherein (and upon the assistance of providence it is to be hoped with many) are concentrated all their hopes, of having an opportunity to escape the devouring element.

After buffetting with the waves, they succeed in reaching the chosen spot, they are now within sixty, nay! perhaps within forty yards of the shore; where numbers of people are assembled, waiting, ready, eager, to afford all possible assistance—and who would willingly go to the wreck, and bring on their backs to the shore, the poor weather-beaten sailors; but alas! they are without their reach. It is true, the distance is small that parts them, but even that small space is occupied by a tremendous enemy,—an angry surf; which awes them to keep at a respectful distance, as tho' it were jealous lest the poor shivering fellows upon the wreck should be rescued from becoming its victims. They now view their situation with horror, for they see no way to *insure* their deliverance; they have not *any means* to accomplish it! they had flattered themselves much from the appearance of the shore,—well—it is not altered—it is the same, and yet invites them to tread its surface; but alas! they are restrained by the impassable gulph that interposes. Though their vessel is on ground, they are afloat on the

waves of doubt and uncertainty; which are big with horror and
dismay! for notwithstanding their case among shipwrecks is not
of the worst sort, yet it is bad; it is dreadful enough to shake
their confidence, and to alarm their fears. They now find themselves exposed to danger, not of the common kind; danger, far sur-
passing in terrors what they had anticipated; for they were before
strangers to shipwreck—only a few on board had experienced it,
and very many had never beheld it with their eyes. In the midst
of heavy storms, they had been accustomed to *float upon* the
" white top wave." But *now* they are frequently enveloped in its
enraged bosom, and covered with its indignant foam. Their fa-
vourite vessel already creaks and cries, and threatens to recede
from their close embraces, by seperating from beneath them—
yet she forbears. The retiring tide favours her keeping together
a little longer—but the poor disconcerted sailors do not heed this
friendly circumstance, their minds are already unhinged—they are
confused in their ideas—distressed in their situation—each one shifts
for himself. The *good swimmer* trusts to his *skill*—the *ordinary*
one marks the *shortness* of the *distance*. The shore is viewed with
anxiety by all—the desperate attempt is undertaken—they plunge
into the sea—they swim—but alas! the ebb tide which favoured
their preservation while upon the wreck, now promotes their destruction! they find it hard work to make any progress towards
the shore—they exert all their strength and skill—they tug hard!
but alas! the breakers too are united against them, and in suc-
cession, with furious dash, beat them to the bottom—they struggle—
most of them struggle their last, and perish! a few only reach the
land.

I believe the foregoing is a faint Delineation of Shipwreck,
in one of its milder forms; however, I purpose to elucidate as I go
on, by briefly relating, or by referring to particulars that have
attended on such melancholy occasions; which will enable my
readers to judge, respecting my ideas and decisions on the subject.

B 2

My residence being within a short distance of the sea, I have had opportunities of witnessing many shipwrecks; among others, that of the ANSON FRIGATE: the leading particulars of which, I will now introduce. The Anson encountered some very heavy weather, and was driven from her station off the coast of France. Seamanship did much, and successfully, to preserve her in the open sea. But the gale continuing with unabated violence, it was deemed prudent to bear up for Falmouth Harbour; unfortunately through the thickness of the weather, she got embayed, a little within the Lizard. Here seamanship again exerted itself to work off, but proved unavailing; she then came to an anchor, and after a few hours she parted; let go another anchor, and after a short time, parted from that also. Very fortunately day-light now enabled the crew to look around them, and survey their situation; when they discovered they could not avoid being wrecked, as the wind was blowing a hard gale—a heavy sea—and the ship not a great distance from the shore. Orders were in consequence given, to select the most promising spot to run on, towards effecting the preservation of their lives; and as the tide had begun to ebb, no time was to be lost. The Loe Pool, Bar of Sand was the chosen spot, & is about the centre of a sandy beach, which extends itself east from Porthleaven Harbour to Gunwallo Fishing Cove, near three miles in length; and is frequently called the long sand. Here the Anson met her fate! The shore being steep, permitted her coming in pretty close before she grounded; and then she took as favourable a position as could be wished, towards promoting the preservation of the people on board, and to facilitate their getting on shore. For, she broached too with her broadside to the sea, and heeled pretty much inwards, thereby checking the fury of the waves, and affording also some shelter from their immediate dash. But notwithstanding the fury of the sea was thus checked, it beat over the ship with violence, frequently flying mast high in a tremendous shower: being thus situated, and the influx of the sea being materially obstructed by such a long solid body as this ship was, (I believe she was a 64 cut down;) a very favourable prospect within, presented itself to the poor fellows on board, who no doubt were eager to escape from the danger to which they were exposed, by putting their feet upon what *they thought* to be firm footing; and which upon the returning back of each wave, *seemed* distant only a *little more than a long Jump.* In the midst of the danger, horror and fear, each one used *his own judgment,* how he should escape from his perilous situation: so being urged on by *terror* from behind, and allured by the flattering prospect which was before them, great numbers jumped overboard; impressed no doubt with the idea, that the shore was within their grasp, and that a very ordinary swimmer would not have to use much exertion to gain it; but soon—very soon, the greatest part of them lost their lives through their mistake! many were immediately swallowed up and seen no more; others, with the out-haul of the sea, or the eddy formed by the ebbing of the tide, were carried with violence round the ship—disappeared—and no doubt were presently dashed to pieces! The loss of lives on this melancholy occasion, was computed at full one hundred, including the brave commander.

From my description of the situation of the Anson, with the addition of her bedding steady in the sand, and holding firmly together; every one who knows (or can conceive,) any thing of shipwreck, will be led to see that the case was not a desperate one; and also, that as the tide had some hours to ebb, the situation of the people upon the wreck was every minute improving. To those who are on shore in peace and *safety,* it must appear strange, that any of the crew (however ignorant or timid,) should have been blind, or insensate to the friendly circumstance of the tide ebbing, which was so plainly working to favour their escape, as fast as time would permit. It must be supposed however, that many on board duly considered this, and prudently waited for the opportunity; as after the water had somewhat receded, the greater part of those that were saved, came ashore without much difficulty upon the main mast, which lay over the side; and by the same method

several persons from the shore went on board. This circumstance
of itself, fully proves, to all human probability, how easily and
safely the poor fellows who jumped overboard, might have been
preserved, had they stuck by the ship.

In this statement plainly appear the weakness and incompetency of man's strength and skill, when in conflict with a foaming surf; and also, that those who trusted their safety to swimming
rushed into the destruction, they were so anxiously striving to
avoid.

But let not blame be heaped upon the heads of the poor
sufferers, no doubt but *they thought* they were doing for *the best :*
although it *cannot* but be *evident*, they acted in error, most fatal
error! and I will endeavour to prove, (I trust successfully,) from
what *cause* their error had its source.

It has already been said, that shipwreck even in its mildest
form, is big with horror; then surely in its more angry and complicated form, language itself must fail to express, with what it is
big. Thus much may be conceived, that it is big with every distress and torment that can possibly assail the minds of men.

The minds of the same men, are more or less affected by the
appearance of danger; as in a more or less degree, it may be armed
with terrors. But under the same circumstances,—exposed to the
same dangers,—various minds, are variously affected; and this can
easily be accounted for, from *constitution* and from *habit*. Such
are the natural constitutions of men, that an occurrence which
will scarcely warm the feelings of some, will melt others down;
dangers which hardly move the apprehensions of some, overcome
others with dismay. Hence, men act more or less composed, or
more or less hastily, in proportion, as *their* respective minds are
operated upon. Whence proceeds a reason, *why* some rush into
destruction, when assailed by danger; while others who are not

so precipitate, and are more collected, are preserved : their respective *feelings* and *actions*, as *causes* and *effects* being perfectly
in unison with each other.

Habit or custom, operates most powerfully, to alter or to
subdue the natural feelings of men.   Hence, sailors get inured to
hardships, and to dangers; whether they proceed from storms or
battles : with storms the more timid become familiar & reconciled,
because of their frequent occurrence.   But although a few year's
experience upon the seas, makes men familiar with the blowing of
the winds, and with the roaring of the waves; yet, a great number
of those experienced hands, are as unacquainted with the nature of
shipwreck, and its attendant miseries, as those who never saw the
ocean, or "the tall ship sailing on the azure seas," and for this reason,
because they never experienced, or perhaps never saw one; consequently are liable to be terrified, in common with others, and are
urged on " to escape for their lives,"—by jumping over board,—or
taking to the boats,—being both alike dangerous, desperate measures, in a stormy sea.

By way of elucidating with what a variety of awful, and
distracting ideas and impressions, the minds of poor creatures en-
during the horrors of shipwreck are exposed to ; and of convincing
my readers of the fatal effects consequent thereon, I will introduce
a few extracts from the narratives of such melancholy occurrences.

Extract from the narrative of the loss of H. M. S. RAVEN,
"To describe would baffle the efforts of the ablest pen—the groans
shrieks and cries of men threatened with instant destruction,—no
hope of saving life; blowing, raining, and dreadfully dark; sea
after sea dashing over us ; the crashing of the falling masts ; and
the shocks which the vessel received in striking the ground, presented nothing short of instant dissolution!

Extract from the narrative of the loss of the VRYHEID,
"Universal consternation now prevailed——the shrieks of the

females and children, at each successive blast of wind, were sufficient to un-man the stoutest heart. Many of the ladies were by
this time, clinging round their husbands & fainting in their arms!"

Extract from the narrative of the loss of H. M. S. NAMUR
" It is easier to conceive than to describe, what a dismal scene
now presented itself——the shriekings, cries, lamentations, ravings,
despair, of above five hundred poor wretches verging on the brink
of eternity."

We here discover the Raven's people (who no doubt were
as brave fellows as others in our navy—and had been accustomed
to meet the foe in battle with a hearty cheer—and to bear with
fortitude and courage, every danger of a storm while a float,) now
uttering " *groans, shrieks* and *cries !*" And on board the Vryheid,
"*universal* consternation, &c. &c." And the Namur's people
possessed by every distress and agony.

Now—for men thus circumstanced—thus affected—to err in
judgment—either in the choice of the *means themselves*, or the *time
of using* them, towards effecting their preservation, is not at all to
be wondered at. And indeed, if being surrounded by such excessive dangers and agonizing distresses, will not drive men to distraction and despair—and deprive them of their wonted powers—
it is not easy to discover what will.

Capt. Fellowes of the LADY HOBART Packet, (when
speaking of her loss) says, "Men accustomed to vicissitudes are
not soon dejected : but, there are trials which human nature alone
cannot surmount.

It may readily be discovered then, that the erroneous acts
of persons encountering Shipwreck, (either in the means they
devise, or in the *time* of *using* them, towards effecting their escape)
are in consequence of the impressions made upon their minds, by

the scene that surrounds them. Nor is it *danger itself* (generally speaking,) that so excessively discomposes them; but, *their not having any means to make use of, upon which they can rely, to se-cure their deliverance.* It is not being *simply* "threatened with destruction," that so much affects their minds,—alarms their fears, and "*un-mans their stout hearts,*"—no it is not this,—for, to dan-ger they have often been exposed; by destruction, they have often been threatened,—both in storm and battle. But "no hope to escape—no hope of saving life; *this* is the *source—this* is the *grand moving cause.*

Since having put my ideas to paper, on this part of the subject, I have read the narrative of the loss of H. M. S. WAGER. The following extract will further illustrate, how men's minds are acted upon in time of shipwreck; and substantiate what I have advanced upon that head. "In this dreadful situation, the ship lay for some time, every soul on board looking upon each suc-ceeding minute as his last; for there was nothing but breakers to be seen all around us. ＊ ＊ ＊ ＊ ＊ ＊ In this terrifying and critical juncture, to have observed all the *various sensations* of horror operating, according to the *several characters* and *dispositions* among us, it was necessary that the observer himself, should have been free from all impressions of danger. There were instances however, of behaviour so very remarkable, that they could not escape the notice of any one who was not entirely bereft of his senses; for some were, to all intents and purposes, in that con-dition. One man in particular was seen stalking about the deck, flourishing a cutlass over his head, calling himself king of the country, &c. Some reduced by long sickness and scurvy, on this occasion became petrified, as it were, and bereft of all sense, and were bandied to and fro, like inanimate logs, by the jerks and rol-ling of the ship, without exerting any efforts to help themselves. So terrible was the scene presented by the foaming breakers around us, that one of the *bravest* men we had, could not forbear expres-sing his dismay, saying it was too shocking a sight to bear; and

c

would even have thrown himself off the rails of the quarter deck into the sea, had he not been prevented. But at the same time, there was not wanting some who preserved a presence of mind truly heroic. Mr. Jones, Mate, (who not only survived this wreck, but likewise that of H. M. Ship, Litchfield, on the coast of Barbary,) at the time when the ship was in the most imminent danger, not only shewed himself undaunted, but endeavoured to inspire the same resolution into the men, by saying, ' My friends, let us not be discouraged ; did you never see a ship among breakers before? let us endeavour to push through them. Come lend a hand, here is a sheet, and there is a brace, lay hold. *I don't doubt but we may stick her near enough to the land to save our lives.*' This address had such a good effect, that many, who were before half dead, seemed active again, and went to work in earnest. On the part of Mr. Jones, however, it was merely intended to *keep up their spirits;* for he himself frequently said afterwards, he thought there was not *the least chance of a single man's life being saved.*"

. This extract clearly elucidates how terribly men's minds are wrought upon by the terrors of shipwreck ; and *particularly* so, by " expecting each succeeding minute to be the last,"—by the prospect of "*not the least chance* of a single life being saved."

Extract from Captain Campbell's Shipwreck. " The vessel which drifted all this time with the sea and wind, gradually approached the shore, and at length struck the ground, which for an instant revived our almost departed hopes ; but we soon found that it did not in the smallest degree better our situation. Again I began to yield to *utter despair.* Again I thought of letting go my hold, and sinking at once. It is impossible thought I, ever *to escape*—why then prolong for a few minutes, a painful existence that must at last be given up ?" again, " death seemed inevitable : and all that occurred to me now to do, was to accelerate it, and get out of its pangs as speedily as possible : for though I knew how to

swim, the tremendous surf rendered swimming useless, & all hope
from it would have been ridiculous."

   Captain Campbell throughout his shipwreck, and succeeding sufferings, evinced that he possessed a resolute mind; yet he
could not but be sensible of the great danger he was exposed to;
and to expect deliverance from *swimming was ridiculous*. He then
proceeds, " I therefore began to swallow as much water as possible; yet, still rising by the buoyant principle of the waves to the
surface, my former thoughts began to revive, and whether it was
that, or natural instinct, which survived the temporary impressions
of despair, I know not, but I endeavoured to swim. I had often
heard it said in Scotland, that if a man will throw himself flat on
his back in the water, lie quite straight and stiff, and suffer himself to sink till the water gets into his ears, he will continue to
float. This occurred to me now, and I determined to try the experiment; so I threw myself on my back in the manner I have
described, and left myself to the disposal of providence; nor was
it long before I found the truth of the saying,—for I floated with
hardly an effort, and began for *the first time* to conceive something
like hopes of preservation. In a short time, without effort or
exertion, and without once turning off my back, I found myself
strike against the sandy beach." I have added this extract from
the narrative, as *information* to my readers, if any of them should
be reduced to the extremity of Captain Campbell, that they may
try the experiment.

   Seeing in the foregoing extracts, how the *several characters*
and *dispositions* were affected, it may reasonably be inferred that
the Anson's people were wrought upon in a corresponding manner.
Why so many jumped overboard, to a certainty was, with a view
to save themselves: but whether their situation on the wreck, was
so terrifying to their minds, as to deprive them of the advantages
of reflection; or whether their general ignorance of shipwrecks,
urged them to the hazardous undertaking, is not for me to say.

But it is very probable, that their *precipitancy* might have proceeded from both causes; some being influenced by the one, and some by the other. There cannot be a question, however, on many of them being allured by the flattering appearance within, to adopt that method of escape, which to them *seemed so ready* and *practicable*; but in the trial, proved so very fatal.

In the evening of that destructive day (the survivors having been marched into this town in their way to Falmouth,) I had some conversation with the boatswain, and expressed my wonder at the eagerness of the men to attempt their preservation by jumping overboard, especially as the tide was ebbing; and made some observations on the dangerous nature of the sand, &c. "Ah!" he replied, "they were a parcel of *Greenhorns*; they were not aware of what they were doing: but I plainly saw what their eagerness to escape, would lead to." In further conversation he told me, he had been wrecked three times.

Having exemplified how excessively men's minds are wrought upon by the terrors attending shipwreck, and that in such discomposed and deranged state, they must necessarily misjudge and misdo, and consequently facilitate their own destruction; I purpose now to shew that experienced sailors, who are not altogether ignorant of the nature of shipwrecks; may even coolly and deliberately, run themselves into the same common ruin with others, through their being *allured* by the fine appearance of a beach, and the short distance from it, to trust their safety to their skill in swimming. It cannot be supposed that *all* the poor fellows belonging to the Anson, who fell victims to their confidence in swimming, and other supposed abilities to reach the shore, were alike unacquainted with the nature of shipwrecks; or that they were alike inconsiderate, respecting the power of the water;—but, it would appear, that they were all alike unacquainted with the nature of the *sand* they were upon. Their ignorance of this, (to a certainty) proved the destruction of many of them.

I do not hesitate to believe, that the Lee Bar of Sand, affords a most pleasing appearance to sailors, who are in the bay in distress; with no prospect of being able to avoid going ashore. The Anson chose this spot, and so have many—very many vessels within my recollection. I also believe that the stiffness of the shore, allowing vessels to come so close in, before take the ground, is an advantage towards saving the people's lives; provided, they have a rope prepared, and can use *means*, *immediately* on grounding, to convey an end of it to those on shore. But without *immediate assistance*, the heavy breakers are big with destruction, as I conceive they must be upon all stiff shores. In addition to the tremendous power of the breakers on this *long sand*, the *sand itself* powerfully co-operates in the work of destruction. To strangers and incautious persons, the sand is very deceiving; and if in case of shipwreck, jumping overboard, and swimming alone is relied on,—ten chances to one but destruction will ensue. The sand being large and loose, the surface of it is put in motion by the run of the waves,—so that supposing a man by his strength and skill in swimming, should escape being swallowed up at first in deep water,—and should be thrown up so far on the sand by the run of a wave, as for his body to be scarcely covered, when lying flat in a swimming position; yet, from the descent of the shore, and the looseness of the sand, he would be hurried again into the breakers by the back-run of the water, (or what our fishermen term the *out-haul*.) Supposing he should be so far possessed of his reason and strength, as to be able to use renewed exertions; and should be thrown in again by another wave, & even get upon his feet, he would quickly find himself in his former dilemma, by the out-haul carrying away the sand from beneath his feet, and again forcing him among the breakers.

It must not be overlooked that the stiffness of the shore adds much to the power of the returning back-water, which, if only a foot in depth, is very great; and it is astonishing with what rapidity the sand is carried away from under a person's feet; which throws him off his legs—when he becomes in jeopardy immediately, and has a very poor chance to escape drowning; unless prompt assistance is afforded. Hence it is that so many of those in the neighbourhood get drowned, or have hair breadth escapes from drowning—when "*a wrecking.*" A few years ago an instance occurred which will elucidate: At a wreck, several persons not sufficiently guarded, were surrounded by the run of a large wave; four were thrown off their legs and carried away,—they were however, all cast in again by the following wave—three of them had immediate assistance, and were saved; but the fourth, was floated out again by the *out-haul* in a sitting posture, and slid along as regular and smoothly as though he had been sitting on an inclined piece of ice; he was hurried in this manner, into the *truck*, from whence alas! there was no return. A young man at the wreck of the *Resolution Brig*, at Porthleaven, last January, was drowned in the same way; entirely owing to his being a stranger to the sand, and to the dangerous nature of it.

Several instances (were they necessary) might be produced for further proof, of the tendency of loose sands *to destroy*. I will presume however on the acceptance of the following anecdote as related by the person himself, only a few days since.

"I was at the wreck of the Anson, and on coming to the spot, found there were only a few of the crew remaining on board. As I was never backward in using my endeavours to save poor shipwrecked sailors, I immediately set about to assist in getting them to land: but knowing the dangerous nature of the sand, I was cautious how I exposed myself to be caught in the surf. I observed a rope fastened to the ship and several persons on the beach holding on the end of it. By this rope I held, and approached nearly under the side of the ship; which I was enabled to do, by the tide having considerably ebbed, and much sand being thrown up just inside the ship, by the sea coming round at each end; and the run of the sea being also checked by such a long vessel, the sand abreast of the wreck was nearly dry. I went in as far as I could, and soon had a *child* handed to me; and Mr. R. at the same time, had one handed to him also; when we immediately made towards the shore. I carried the child under one arm, and held by the rope with the other: Mr. R. was a few yards from me. I begged him to take the assistance of the rope, in like manner to myself; he said no,—he could do without it. I then urged him saying, you have not been to so many wrecks as I have,—nor are you acquainted with the run of the sea—or the nature of the sand! No! no! he could do very well. At this moment a tremendous large sea, ran far in upon the beach at each end of the ship, and met within us; so we were inclosed by the returning water. As I was holding by the rope I sustained myself; but Mr. R. was washed off his legs: I saw his danger, but feared if I quitted my rope, I should get into the same predicament. My apprehensions however, for his safety, and for that of the child, prevailed; I ran the risk, (being a tall man) and seized him by the collar, and succeeded in getting him upon his legs again; or I do not doubt, but both he and the child, would have been drowned."

Persons who are strangers to such a shore, as I have been enlarging upon—who are strangers to the nature of a stormy sea, and to shipwreck; will feel their surprize at so many lives being lost—increased—at being told, that several vessels have grounded so close to the shore, as to afford the people there assembled, the opportunity of throwing a rope to the wreck, to assist the people from it. (Several of the fishermen at Porthleaven who have assisted on those occasions, can testify to this.) Now observe,—notwithstanding vessels come in so close before take the ground,—yet, without the assistance of a rope, destruction is almost inevitable, for the aforesaid reasons,—the power of the breakers—and the looseness of the sand. The fishermen being aware of this, (from having had many melancholy instances,) and also, that the sailors in general are not able to throw a rope to the shore (either through not having one prepared, or from being overcome with terror,)

frequently take this necessary article with them, when they see a
vessel coming ashore; that *they* may have the means of opening a
communication, when *possibility* admits of it: for it cannot be
done on *every* part of the beach, *every* period of the tide, nor to
vessels of a large class.

I remember witnessing (several years ago,) a Danish Brig
to part from her anchors in Porthleaven Bay. She immediately
hoisted a *jib* and a *stay-sail*, and ran in before the wind, upon this
long sand; the people on the shore, by hallooing and waving their
hats, directed her to an eligible spot. On grounding, she immediately broached to with her broadside to the sea; and the crew
very promptly threw out the end of a rope. This was obliged to
be repeated several times before the people on shore could get hold
of it; but as soon as they did, the crew successively applied it to
their bodies,—threw themselves overboard,—and were soon hauled
to the shore. The captain was the last man that quitted the wreck,
and while he was putting the rope around him, a large sea broke
upon the vessel, by which he was overwhelmed. He disappeared
for a small space, and we thought he was washed overboard; fortunately he was only struck down and stunned, he soon recovered
himself and was saved as the others were. The vessel had begun
to break up, while her crew were yet on board: a few minutes
more before the rope was got hold of—and it would have been too
late. In half an hour after she struck, she was all in pieces, and
her cargo floating in every direction.

To further illustrate what I have been advancing, about the
destructive nature of this sand, I will relate that a foreign vessel
stranded on the Loe Bar, some little time after the Anson. On
coming in, the crew it would appear, had not made any *provision*
towards even *trying* to get the end of a rope ashore; perhaps
they had not conceived the stiffness of the beach, was so great as
to have admitted of their coming in so close as to render it *possible*:
or they might have been flattered into ideal security, by the fine

appearance of the sand ; and put confidence in swimming. However when she struck, they were unprepared to throw a rope ashore,— or were so overcome with the terrors of their situation, that they *could not.* The vessel being a weak one, *directly* went to pieces ; and notwithstanding the exertions of the many, who were assembled on the beach, only *two* out of *eleven* were saved.

The French Brig, Hermacon, lost on the same sand, a little farther to the east of the foregoing ; is another proof. Read the narrative for particulars.

It appears pretty clearly that *swimming* in case of ship-wreck, very seldom affords preservation,—and that trusting to it, very often hastens destruction. I shall now proceed briefly to shew, that the use of *boats* affords a source for preservation, very little superior to that of *swimming.*

It is frequently the case that vessels during a storm lose their boats, or get them rendered unfit for service—in either of these cases, they *cannot* be had recourse to : but when they have been preserved, and vessels running aground in heavy weather, have made use of them,—it appears, in a far *greater number* of instances, they have assisted only to accelerate destruction.

Blanche, Frigate, lost on the coast of France, 1807.—"A few hands got into the quarter boats, and they were no sooner on the water, than they were dashed to pieces!"

Barbadoes, lost 10th October, 1816, on the rocks of Scilly.—"The Captain and fifteen men took to two boats, which soon upset, and all perished!"

A Boat which had been on the look-out for vessels near Gorleston, October 8th, 1816, in attempting to come in, was upset in the surf, and only two out of eight were saved.

D

Jane and Rebecca.—A boat was lowered with four seamen, and lost.

Lord Melville, Transport.—" A boat was launched and manned with five sailors: two officers, two ladies, and some others got into it; it was soon swamped, and only one of the sailors was saved ! "

Litchfield, Man of war.—" A boat was got out, and eight of the best seamen got into her, but she had scarcely got to the ship's stern, when she was whirled to the bottom, and every soul in her perished ! "

Solptre, Man of war.—" The launch was now hoisted out, but was unfortunately upset, and totally lost with the whole of her crew ! "

Vryheid.—" At the earnest request of the Admiral, the jolly boat (which was hanging over her stern,) was now launched ; and he, together with the Colonel, and eight females were helped into it. They had not proceeded far, when a dreadful sea broke over her,—and she instantly disappeared !—In a few moments the Colonel was seen endeavouring to support his lady above water—when a returning wave overwhelmed them, and they rose no more ! "

These are a few among the many instances that I could produce from what have occurred in this neighbourhood, and recorded in narratives of shipwrecks, to prove that the use of boats in severe weather, affords a very *precarious* means of preservation at best ; is always very *hazardous* ; and frequently big with certain destruction.

Seeing then that the horrors, and that the destruction of human life, attendant upon shipwreck are so very extreme ;—and that the consequent miseries and distresses which are entailed upon surviving relatives and friends are incalculable;—what rational creature but must feel deeply interested, in the fate of those who traverse the wide ocean?

As men, and all proceeding from the power of the same Creator;—as men,—and all being descendants of the same original parents;—it cannot but be presumed, there is not a nation upon the face of the whole earth (the uncivilized only excepted,) but feels serious concern for the welfare of those, who, in the course of providence, are called to travel upon the surface of the trackless great deep.

To *prevent* Shipwreck, is not in the power of mortals;—but to *lessen* its *calamities*, by the assistance of providence, is within our reach. This is believed:—and to accomplish it, efforts have been made—means have been devised. But alas! hitherto these means have been all *ineffective!!* *Preservation* to shipwrecked sufferers, have been afforded in a very partial,—very limited,—very confined way. Of this, proofs—incontrovertible proofs,—have been abundant every winter; but especially the last, which has been fruitful indeed in shipwrecks, all along our coasts; with *loss of lives in melancholy numbers.*

It is however a happy circumstance, for all those who traverse the wide ocean, whether mariner or passenger, that *an Apparatus is now invented,* and a plan devised, which is capable of affording them very extensive assistance when overtaken by distress,—by day, or by night; and almost in any situation, or under any circumstance. Nor is its utility confinable to vessels driven ashore—but extends itself to afford succour, even " in the midst of the sea"—and that too, when severity of weather, precludes the use of ordinary means.

I have already said that I have had opportunities of witnessing several melancholy wrecks, and among others, that of the

D 2

Anson, Frigate, when about one hundred of her crew were lost; to their country, as brave defenders; and to their own connections, as beloved relatives and friends.

As however, sometimes it happens, that *good* comes out of *evil*,—so I flatter myself, that this great loss, will ultimately be productive of a great blessing to the whole world!—For, by it (in addition to the premature destruction of about fifty at the wreck of the Jane and Rebecca, Transport, in this neighbourhood, only a few weeks preceding) my mind was so affected, as to be led into a train of reflection and reasoning on the melancholy catastrophe, as to be very soon possessed by the idea of devising means, to be used as a *Life Preserver*.

Thus then, this wreck, which was so very destructive to human life, *gave birth* to my Life Preserving Apparatus; and so powerfully did the impulse operate upon my mind, as almost wholly to engross it. Nor has it once entered into my thoughts, but the means I was studying to contrive, must be kept on shipboard, to be rendered useful.

I soon fixed on a *Preserver* of such description as might certainly have been used at the wreck of the Anson * to advantage.

At that time I think I had only *three* methods to convey a line to land. The first was a *Piece* of *Lead* † resembling a half

* This Preserver might have been useful at this wreck,—but I now see, that it could be useful only at the wrecks of large vessels, when aground very close to the shore. It was defective, especially by wanting portability.

† This method is undoubtedly adequate to open a communication, when a vessel runs on a stiff shore:—instance—such as where the Anson did. It was proved to be adequate at the wreck of the Amicus—(which refer to.) When I devised the method, I had not heard of Mr. Giles, or the loss of the Amicus,—(which happened about the time the Anson was lost,) consequently I could not

pound weight, with a hole through it to receive the end of the line; to be thrown by a man's hand,

The second method (and which I then placed much confidence in) was a *Kite*. *

The third method was the use of *a Rocket*. †

A model of the Preserver, and a written description, I shewed to a gentleman in this neighbourhood; who shewed it to a friend of his, (who had formerly belonged to the Admiralty,) and they both agreed that the invention was entitled to *consideration*.

The former gentleman caused it to be transmitted to Government, after which I heard no more about it. Probably, the bustle

---

borrow the scheme. It was only very lately, in reading the Mariner's Chronicle, that it came to my knowledge of having been ever used,

* It would appear there is much plausibility attached to the method of using a Kite: because various persons, not known to each other, have recommended it. As respects date, I have the precedence. I recollect that a letter appeared in a newspaper, between one and two years ago, (I think in the St. James's Chronicle,) from a Naval Officer, addressed to the Mayor of Exeter, on the subject of conveying a rope from a wreck to land; and requesting that the method might be made known along the coast, from thence to Plymouth. The method was the use of a Kite. Doctor Muter also recommends the method; see his letter at the latter end. Some in this neighbourhood, have thought on the same scheme.—Last year, going to the wreck of the Young Autony, Dutch Galliot; an acquaintance of mine on the road, pointed out a Kite as an excellent conveyance: and another since then—but for myself—I have relinquished it long since, as a too uncertain method.

† Doctor Muter says, "I am convinced from the experiments I have made with the Rocket, that it can be used with the greatest promptitude, and at a distance from the shore much greater than that to which the Mortar (in Captain Manby's plan) of the largest size is limited."

created by the war, in the naval department;—and my not having
made a single experiment with any part of the apparatus, to ascertain its *practicability*, as a recommendation for its adoption; might
have been two reasons why it was not attended to.

Several months now passed without my *hearing*, or doing
any thing about it; but my feelings were as much as ever alive, to
the object I had in view—the impressions made on my mind were
not in the least diminished, although I did not succeed in my first
effort; and I proceeded under the unaltered convictions, that
whatever it might be my scheming should produce, it must be such,
as would allow of its becoming a portable part of a ship's equipment: and I clearly saw, that on opening a communication with
promptitude, from the wreck with the shore, every benefit depends.
To ascertain effectual means to accomplish this desirable object, I
tried many expedients; but gave preference to the rocket, and
some methods of using a musket. With these, I made various experiments, and with various success. I was convinced that the
principle of my methods was good, and adhered to my plan; but
being very peculiarly circumstanced, by a train of personal, and
family afflictions;—many preventatives interposed to my pursuing
the subject, so closely as I wished. (Hence the lapse of time.)
However, after much perseverance, and renewed efforts in making
experiments with those methods, I have *now* so far succeeded in
obtaining a knowledge of the use of them, as to be prompted to
believe there is not *another man* in the *United Kingdoms*, who can
project a line to *equal distance*, and with *equal precision* and
promptitude, with *any description* of Apparatus, that is of equal
portability to my own, and which is not on the *same principle*.
On this I am satisfied in my own mind, and do not fear refutation.

The line * I project, is adequate to draw a rope to the

---

* The projecting line, I expect, is strong enough to haul a man through
the water, for it is larger than whip cord, which Mr. Giles used for that pur-

shore, sufficiently large, to be used as a *hauling rope ;* to haul persons *through* the water, or *above* the water, on a hawser. If through the water, then a FLOAT * is to be affixed to the rope,

---

pose at the wreck of the Amicus. But a rope is preferable for two reasons,— because there should be no risk : and, because in cold and wet, a rope can be handled better than a line.

* The most general method made use of by those on shore, to assist persons from a wreck, (when circumstances do favour communication,) is to haul them through the water by a rope. In this manner, or by this method, they must unavoidably be exposed to sinking in the water, and also to the fury of its agitated state. They are thus dragged along, continually sousing and thumping against the bottom,—being unmercifully beat down by the tremendous dash of every wave. If the shore is flat, the wreck will take the ground at some considerable distance, with a long run of surf within :—so that in the very act of saving men, they nearly perish from drowning, and from bruises. Of the truth of this, many proofs have been afforded in this neighbourhood. Some time since a foreign vessel was stranded on Praah Sand, about midway between this and Marazion, which being flat, she grounded from 100 to 150 yards from the shore. The tide favouring the floating a rope to land by a buoy, the aforesaid method was made use of; and all the crew were thus brought from the wreck, in an exhausted and almost lifeless state.

A large ship stranded near Hayle, a few years since, on a flat sand, and the crew were hauled in the same way through the water ; and when brought to land were nearly lifeless. The person who related this to me said he was an eye witness, and that some of them were under water for several minutes; and two of them died.

Being sensible from my own observations, that this way of saving lives, is putting the poor unfortunate sufferers by a rout, very near to death's door ; I wished to find out some better one;—and this led to the contrivance of my Float. The use of the Float completely obviates the misery attached to the common way as described, by its buoyancy not permitting the person having it on to sink ; for it is buoyant enough to float the largest person breast high.

It appears from the narratives of shipwrecks I have seen, that sailors in general are aware of, or anticipate the miseries attached to the method used by the people from the shore ; and that they have an aversion to it.—For I do

(which may be done in a minute,) and wrapt round the body of
the person to be floated to land, when he will leap into the water,
and be quickly hauled to shore.   On reaching the shore, the Float
must be immediately taken off, and hauled back to the wreck for
the next person; and so on till all are saved.   Provided a stranded
vessel should not go to pieces *directly*, (and circumstances admit,)
a hawser may be hauled taught from the vessel to the shore, on
which a numerous crew may be landed,—comfortably and quickly,
by means of a * CHAISE ROLANTE Conveyancer, suspended
to wheels, † which run upon the hawser; and are so constructed
as to be worked with the most *possible rapidity*, without producing
the least friction.

    With those parts of the Apparatus, I made my first expe-
riments at Porthleaven, now about twelve months since. (It was
the very first time the *Float* was in water, and the very first time
the *Chaise Rolante* was suspended to a rope.   Experiments in projecting a line, it must be understood, I made many before; but
this was the first time of doing it in *public*.)   A great number of

---

not think I have seen one instance recorded, of their having used it; (when they
have not had help from the shore, but have been obliged to help themselves,)
but when they have been able to get a rope ashore, they have used a hawser to
walk on: (as instanced in the loss of the Litchfield,) or to warp themselves
upon, (as in the case of the Grosvenor.)   Although these methods have been
preferred to the other, by sailors themselves, yet their inconveniency and insecurity were fully evidenced, when made use of.   See the narratives.   My Float
when in use, is always fast to the hauling rope.   It is as easily put on, and off
as a man's waistcoat.

    * The Chaise Rolante is so portable, that a child of three years' old
may with ease carry it under his arm.   It is a safe, easy, and indeed a comfortable conveyance, and affords the accommodation of an arm chair; and perfect
security even to infirm, sick, wounded, females, or children.

    † The Wheels are such as a brother of Lord Exmouth, deemed " curi-
ously contrived."

spectators were present, (several of them respectable gentlemen,) to whom general satisfaction was given. A day or two afterwards, I was called upon by Mr. Russell, (with whom I believe I never exchanged words on the subject before, only to tell him, of my intended experiments,) who said " the apparatus so evidently possessed certain means of affording preservation, to the unfortunate shipwrecked ; he thought public testimony should be borne to it : and if I had no objection, he would write a letter to the Editor of one of the Truro Newspapers.". He did so : and so did another respectable person, under the signature of *Spectator*, to the Editor of the other Truro Paper. A few lines from one of them I extract.

"On last friday, Mr. Trengrouse publicly exhibited the use of his apparatus at Porthleaven. From the western shore, he threw several lines across the harbour, which went over the pier, to some distance on the outer side. The length of line projected was about 200 yards. He has so perfected this part of his plan, as certainly to render it superior to every other method. A *Float* made of cork (the advantage of this will immediately appear to any one, who ever witnessed poor fellows dragged by a rope, through the foaming surf, from a wreck to the shore: almost killed by the means made use of to save their lives,) was applied to the body of a man, with his cloaths on, (who volunteered his services though the wind blew hard,) who was presently and comfortably hauled across the harbour, in a perfectly buoyant state. He then made a signal to return by the same means ; and after warming his stomach with a little good brandy,—he took his seat in a *Chaise Rolante*, suspended to a large rope; (which was drawn across the harbour,) and in this, he was conveyed over and back again, in little more than two minutes."

The leading articles of my apparatus, and their purposes, (as relate to the common course of shipwreck,) being thus briefly described ; I shall now refer to the list of melancholy narratives, and shew *where*, and *how*, they might have been applied, *(beyond*

E

the shadow of a doubt) so as to have saved very many lives. I shall refer to the cases as they stand in the list, alphabetically.

The ANSON *Frigate.* As I have enlarged pretty much on the loss of this ship, to exhibit the *nature* of the common course of shipwreck, and to show *how*, and *why*, the loss of lives too generally is excessive: so I purpose to enlarge pretty much on the application of my apparatus to this ship, to exhibit how it may be made instrumental to preserve life.

But First, in looking through the general run of shipwrecks it plainly appears, that many lose their lives through ignorance; many through imprudence, precipitancy, error in judgment, distraction; many through despair, quietly laying themselves down in the arms of overwhelming destruction. Now, by *which* of *these ways* it may be, it proceeds from the same *central cause*; and *that cause* is, the not having any *provision made* against the time of extremity. Their *not having in possession any means* on which they have *reliance to effect preservation.* THIS IS THE CAUSE.

As it is a received maxim, that "no *effect* can rise above its *cause*,"—and also—"*remove* the *cause* and the *effect* will *cease*;" so it will hold good here, that a *preventative* to the *cause*, will necessarily *prevent* the *effects*. A variety of instances concur, to prove the existence of the cause, which has proved so fatal;—and some few, (unfortunately very few indeed,) to prove the *ceasing* of the *effects*, by the *removal* of the *cause*. However, happily I have it in my power to elucidate to a demonstration.

Early in the late war, the Dutton Indiaman, with troops on board, drove on shore in a gale of wind, near Plymouth. From what I can recollect of the account of it, that appeared in the newspapers; and of a representation of the wreck in an engraving I saw soon after the unfortunate occurrence; I conceive, her situation must have been very similar to that of the Anson;—only less distressing—the wind not being so strong, nor the seas so heavy. The situation of the Dutton on grounding, however, was fully proved to be *such,* as to produce all the sensations on the minds of the people on board, which are common on such like occasions. For, disorder, anarchy, and confusion prevailed: all were eager to save themselves—each using his own method, &c. Fortunately Admiral Lord Exmouth (then Captain Pellew,) was present. His penetrating eye soon discovered the destruction that was at hand; and his fertile mind as readily suggested a remedy: a material part of which was to *re-call* the people on board *to order,* and to impress their minds with a *confidence* of being *preserved.* This could be accomplished only by communicating his ideas, and instructions, relative to the means necessary to be used; to do which was the difficulty. There were *no means* of *conveyance:* the roaring of the wind and sea, prevented the sound of the strongest voice from reaching the wreck; and the only expedient that appeared possible, was for a man to *go from the shore!* His Lord-ship endeavoured to procure a man who would undertake the arduous, yet essential task; and offered a handsome sum of money as a stimulous. But the difficulty, and risk, outweighed every other consideration;—all shrunk from it. His Lordship, however, being clearly convinced, that the preservation of a great number of lives depended upon this one thing, nobly *volunteered himself* to the task of humanity; and Providence owning his christian courage succeeded him in getting safely on board. Order was very soon restored, by assuring the people of preservation; and his Lord-ship insisted, there should not an individual quit the ship, but by the means he was about to adopt; and that, in an orderly, regular manner: that *himself* would be the *last* man on board. Ropes were got ashore to effect the work of preservation: I do not re-member the precise means made use of; I believe there was not a life lost after his Lordship got on board.

By this brief narrative of the Dutton's loss, we see how soon the minds of hundreds of people, of both sexes and various

E 2

ages, were *calmed*, by the *assurance* of *deliverance being at hand!*
No disorder, no confusion *now*;—but each one waiting for his
turn ; all consoling themselves with the belief, that a little longer
exposure to the wash of the waves, would be the extent of their
sufferings ; as the means by which their comrades were conveyed
to the shore, would shortly convey them thither in safety also.

While with pleasure we see the great good here produced—
the great preservation here afforded ;—we also see, that it was *con-*
sequent upon Lord Exmouth's going *on board the wreck* : that it
proceeded from the judgment, humanity, and courage of his Lordship ! We may suppose there were many present possessed of
judgment,—many possessed of humanity,—many possessed of courage ; but not *one* in whom these excellencies *manifested* themselves
to be combined, and so eminently possessed, as in, and by, his
Lordship. And while we rejoice at the existence of those excellencies, in one of our distinguished naval commanders ; we discover
that the resulting benefits, all hung upon a casualty :—the *single*
casualty of that individual who possessed them, being *present* at
the *critical moment.*

Now let me ask—what would have been the fate of the
poor creatures who were thus delivered, if Lord Exmouth had not
providentially been upon the spot ? Or if more extreme circumstances rendered going on board impossible ? Or if his Lordship's
health had prevented going into the water ? Or if the Dutton had
gone ashore at any other place, where such a one as his Lordship
was not ? What would have been their fate ? surely it does not
require the spirit of divination to discover ! The tears of hundreds of weeping widows, orphans, parents and friends, would
have published to the world, their melancholy fate !

If then, (as in the case of the Dutton) *promised deliverance*
(though by means to be then hastily contrived and constructed,)
operates on the mind as a *restorative* so powerfully, as to allay the

disquiet and distraction, of such a vast number of souls in the midst
of danger ;—may it not be reasonably expected that *having* a com-
modious, safe, and *Efficient Life Preserver on board*, would prove
an *effectual preventative* to the inroads of those direful intruders ?
As a *preventative* has ever been deemed better than a *remedy*, so
there cannot be a question, but that the *knowledge* of the apparatus being on board the Dutton, would have *kept* the people's
minds, in a far superior state of composure, than it were possible
for any thing to *restore* them to, after they were so extremely dis-
ordered. And being *kept* in a composed state (by *that knowledge*,
of having such preserving means at command,) would have prevented any of them from even attempting to save themselves by
any other way.

How the horrors of shipwreck operate on poor sufferers to
deprive them of their wonted powers, and render them helpless,—or
else precipitate them into destruction ; cannot be better evidenced
than in the extract from the Wager Man of War. Nor can any
thing be more demonstrative of the benefits attendant on a *persuasion* that preservation will be effected—than the effects which
the address of Mr Jones produced upon the Wager's people.

It may justly be inferred, that the Life Preserving Apparatus having been on board the Anson, would have produced the
most happy effects on the minds of the whole crew. For, being
about to run upon such a find sand, where many people were already assembled ; and with the means in their own hands to open
an immediate communication with them ; and such efficacious con-
veyances to transfer them to the shore so speedily and safely ;
surely they could not necessarily have had even their apprehensions
moved.

I will now endeavour to elucidate this, by shewing *how* I
would have managed with the apparatus on board, and having the
command of the ship.

On receiving the Apparatus on board, I would explain its use, and methods of application, to the whole ship's company; and when opportunity offered, I would make a few experiments, by way of convincing them all, of its utility; and should be as particular in requiring the attention of the Officers to it, as to any part of the duties of the service. I should be particular in having two or three, 5 or 6 inch Hawsers so situated, as to be ready for use at a minute's notice; and also that some of the ship's cordage was in the like state, from which, two or three Hauling Ropes, of 200 or 300 yards each, might be taken with promptitude. (I am not sufficiently acquainted with ships of war, to know *their* particular state: but it is very probable that such ropes as I have mentioned, are always at hand. I know they are common enough upon the decks of merchant ships, in coils.) The apparatus chest, (which is only about the size of a seaman's chest,) should be lashed down to the deck. (Perhaps as convenient a place as any for it always to be kept, may be upon the quarter deck, somewhere about,—*abaft the wheel.*) My ship being thus furnished with life preserving means, I should deem it an important part of my duty, that they were kept in a state always fit, & ready to be used on emergency.

On seeing that the Anson's going ashore was inevitable, the deck should be made as clear as possible of every incumbrance. Guns, or any other moveable that could possibly do mischief, by shifting, should be thrown overboard : and to lessen the danger attendant on the rigging falling, I would (as far as possible,) strike top-masts, and lower yards—or even cut some of them away. The ship would then make her way under a sail or two, towards the sand which had such a favourable appearance, and in this state of preparation ;—with such a life preserving apparatus on board ;— and my people all acquainted with its life preserving powers ;—I should approach with the ship towards the Loe Bar, with nearly as much composure, (relative to my own, and to my people's safe-ty,) as though I were going into harbour : and for the same rea-sons I should expect that all on board would feel as easy as myself.

It would then follow as a matter of course, that the same state of discipline would exist throughout the ship, as had been customary in going through the routine of any usual duty.

On coming within a cable's length of the shore, I should put the ship's head so far to the east or west, (as circumstances might incline,) as would bring the wind well on upon her quarter, and run her in upon the sand, in an oblique direction; which would immediately bring her broadside to the sea, and at the same time heel her a little inwards. (As to keep her in this position would be of the greatest importance, perhaps the use of a top stay-sail might prove a good assistant.) Before she came near the shore, the line projecting part of the apparatus should be taken out of the chest, and one of the officers be stationed with it on the forecastle, prepared to project a line as soon as she came sufficiently near; even before she grounded. While the officer was thus prepared to project the line, a man should be standing by, with a hauling rope all clear for paying out—with an end of it in his hand, waiting to fasten it to the line, the instant the projected end reached the shore; which the spectators would immediately lay hold on. Thus a communication would be opened with the people on shore by a *hauling rope*, in the short space of two minutes after she struck. The line which was first projected, might now be used to get two other hauling ropes ashore from the quarter deck; while by the first hauling rope got ashore from the forecastle, the end of a hawser was forwarding; and so with the others, until three hawsers were strained from the ship to the shore, as taught as possibly they could be. A *Chaise Rolante* should then be mounted upon each of the hawsers, (which would require only a very few minutes to do,) by which the crew would all, safely and quickly, be conveyed to land. Each of the officers, (with no inconveniency) might also take his *portable desk* with him, or any other portable property.

As is usual with commanders of ships on such like occasions, I should feel disposed to see all the people safely landed before quit the wreck myself. I should desire a couple of active officers, and a few lusty, active men to tarry with me. By the time the crew would be landed, I calculate the ebbing of the tide, would enable me and my party to move about; when we would look round for what portable property could be got at, which should be sent ashore upon the hawsers, in the same manner as the people were conveyed : and I should not think of quitting the ship while any good could be done in this way, until the flowing again of the tide obliged us. Indeed, some of the country people upon the beach, might be sent on board to assist, if thought necessary—this they would readily have assented to, as they had such a safe retreat open.

This is how I would have acted with the Anson, and I am as fully persuaded of the efficacy of my apparatus, to be adequate to have saved *every individual* of her people (accidents excepted,) as I am persuaded of my own existence. I am firmly of opinion also, that many articles of valuable property might have been got ashore. From the favourable circumstances of her coming in soon after the tide began to ebb, and her keeping firm together ; with her fore and mizen, with their top masts, and bowsprit, all standing till the next flood ;—the whole of the business might have been done very *deliberately*.

AMICUS.—This ship must have been on shore *fourteen* hours before the last of the crew got from the wreck. The Captain, Mate, and at least three others, lost their lives. The case of these unfortunate people is so very plain—further detail, or argument, is quite unnecessary to *prove*, that *every one of them might have been preserved*, in the *early* stage of the wreck, had the APPARATUS been ON BOARD. And probably, some of the most portable property might have been saved also.

BOADICEA.—By the assistance of the night signals comprised in my plan, this very unfortunate vessel on parting her cables, might have been run ashore, on the most eligible spot in the vicinity. And as the apparatus may be used with nearly the same promptitude, and certainty, by night as by day ; *Preservation* might have been afforded in a very extensive degree.

In the course of the day, while this vessel was riding at anchor, the sailors, by signals for that purpose, should have informed the people upon the shore, of her state, and of their apprehensions. Or as the residents on the coast, must be acquainted with the nature of the ground she was riding on ; *they* could have drawn their own conclusions respecting her fate. Signals, however, should have been exchanged—the agents for wrecks should have selected the spot, most calculated to facilitate the preservation of the people on board. It should then be ascertained if *rocks*, or *any other things* were adjacent, to which hawsers could be fixed. If *nature* had not supplied those things, then *art* should. Large grapnels, or a small anchor or two, should have been brought to the spot, and put in such places as were most suitable. If these were not at hand, some *posts* should have been got ready to force into the ground. All this should have been done in the day time ; and if after all, this preparation was not called into use, through the vessel weathering out the storm ; the labour & expence would have been trifling, and much reason would have been for rejoicing, that she had escaped the horrors of shipwreck. But as it turned out, all the preparations would have been very seasonable, against her coming ashore ; every man would have been at his post, ready to do his part of the work; in affording preservation. On board the unfortunate floating barrack, the numerous inhabitants, would be kept in a great measure composed in their minds, by the knowledge of life preserving means being at hand : every one would be in a state to act coolly and promptly, especially the sailors, who being thus kept free from perturbation, would be *themselves:* which would of itself lead to the most beneficial consequences.

Things being arranged, by signals from the shore, the sailors would have been enabled to run the vessel upon the spot selected.

F

Two or three lines might have been instantly projected to the shore
by means of rockets; by the light of which, the people would
have been able to get hold of them instantly; when the further
process would have been the same, as in the Anson's case. If the
tide was flowing, * the danger of her going to pieces would be
great; and the situation altogether of the vessel and people, extremely perilous; then, *all the Floats* on board should be in use,
as well as every *Chaise Rolante*, on the hawsers. Thus, the far
greater part, if not all of the 220 who perished, might have been
preserved to their country, and to their friends. Of this I have
no doubt.

BARBADOES.—Signals might have informed the people
on the shore. And as by my methods, a line may be projected to
a very considerable distance; I am of opinion that assistance
might have been afforded. The particulars of this wreck I am not
acquainted with, I cannot therefore venture to make positive
assertions.

BLUE BONNET.—I consider it as very probable (from
the ways and means contained in my plan,) that preservation
might have been afforded to those who were on board this ill-fated
vessel.

CHASSE MAREE.—I do not doubt but all the crew
might have been saved.

DROITS DE L'HOMME.—The wreck of this ship was
attended with such extreme horror, distress, and misery; and
finally with such an excessive—unparalleled destruction of human

---

* It might perhaps have been a very wise and prudent measure, as so
many lives were at stake, not to have trusted to the casualty of the anchors
and cables holding; but have cut, and run ashore, just after the tide had
begun to ebb.

life,—as to cause my feelings to rise above my powers of expression. But I may be permitted to say, that accounts of such vast
numbers of my fellow creatures, being prematurely hurried into
eternity ; do cause my heart to burn with anxious desire, for the
adoption of my life preserving apparatus. I beg to refer my readers to the narrative of this wreck, and they will easily discover
the benefits, the apparatus would have afforded.—Very probably,
the enormous number of 1000 lives might have been saved !

DIAMOND.—Had this vessel, or the Hornet Schooner,
got the apparatus on board, a line might have been conveyed from
one to the other to a certainty : and by the use of one or two
Floats, every one of the people might have been transferred from
the wreck to the Hornet in safety.

DANISH SHIP.—The crew might have been saved by the
Orpheus directly, on falling in with her the first time, had the a
paratus been on board.

DISPATCH Transport.—It is very probable by the night
signals, and means contained in the plan ; the people on the shore
might have been informed, and have rendered assistance so as to
have saved the greater part, if not all on board.

GROSVENOR East Indiaman.—As only a few individuals
belonging to this unfortunate ship, survived the calamities attendant
on the wreck, to return to their native land to tell their sad tale ;
and as East Indiamen carry a great number of men ; and frequently many passengers, who in time of shipwreck (as in the
case before me—*seeing no prospect of escaping*,) would not hesitate
to pay for a *ship-load* of *Apparatus*, to effect their preservation,
with that of their wives and children, could it be *obtained at such
a price* :—I will apply the use of my Apparatus and plan to this
wreck, pretty fully.

F 2

First,—be it understood, I calculate on the whole ship's company having the knowledge of the apparatus being on board ; and of its extensive preserving means; as in case of the Anson described. On the Grosvenor running upon the rocks so unexpectedly, *surprise*, and *consternation* would necessarily possess the minds of the people : But, "*distraction* and *despair*," would be kept far away—*because* there would not be any avenue for *its* approach. "*Mothers would not be lamenting over their children*, and *husbands* over both," on account of destruction having *appeared* on the ballance of their existence ; *because*, they would be *sensible* they had a *counterpoise* in their possession. "Anarchy and confusion" could not make *their* appearance on board, therefore could not take possession of the ship. But *Discipline* and *Order*, (instead of wasting time in "*devising*," and in "*constructing*," the most *probable* methods :"—yet " *terrific*,—*difficult*,—*hazardous*,"—nay, in themselves *destructive !*) would serenely and collectedly—promptly and confidently, *apply* the *Specific Remedy*, which (under providence,) they knew was put into their possession.

Being upon a strange coast, and no one in view upon the shore, the first thing to be done, would be for a good swimmer to put on a Float, and proceed with a line to land. I say a *good swimmer*, because, he would by his skill, be able to perform his task in much less time, than one who did not know how to propel himself forward in the water. The man having landed with the line, (I will suppose it to be the very identical deep sea line, which was really carried to land from the Grosvenor,) he should assist two or three men with floats on, by that line, to come ashore from the ship ; they, bringing with them the end of a hauling rope.— With this rope, the three or four on the shore, should haul a hawser, fasten the end of it to the rocks, and have it strained by the capstan. (as was really done.) The hawser being thus strained, a *Chaise Rolante* should be immediately mounted, and an officer sent ashore to direct in the future operations. Six or eight men should then be landed to assist in working. The females, children

and sick, should follow after. (Each of those on board who had
children, might take a child on their lap, in their passage to land,
with ease and safety.) While this work was going forward, the
end of a two inch rope should be sent to land, by one of the men
in his passage by the Chaise Rolante; to be used as an *assistant* to
save the *Boats.* A boat should then be got ready for launching,
and before put over the ship's side, should have a sail folded into
her, with the top fold of it, over-lapping the gunnel, to which it
should be tacked; this would serve as a *deck* and would prevent
her filling, in her passage to the shore. The rope should then be
fastened to the bow of the boat, (and passed through the ring-bolt
at the stern, if deemed advantageous) when she should be launched
and by a preconcerted signal, as soon as she was afloat the people
upon the shore should pull with all their strength, and haul her to
land. The boat being secured, the rope should be cast off, and
hauled back by the people on board, (those on shore retaining
only a few yards of the end of it,) and the other boats sent to land
in the same way: sending in them masts, sails, oars, &c. The
success attending the passage of the first boat, would determine on
what stores could be sent in the others. By this method I *confidently presume* on the preservation of the *Boats.* (Refer to the
loss of the Ingebord Yacht; and see how the advantages of *a rope*
were evidenced.)

Immediately on its being ascertained that the ship had stuck
fast, attention should be directed towards such things, as would be
necessary to the people's *future* preservation. The Gunner should
lose no time in securing some arms and ammunition; the Carpenter should be as active to secure his tool-chest, &c. Three or four
sails should be bound up each in a bundle; provisions, bread, water, compass, quadrant, small cordage, fish hooks, tinder-box, &c.
should be sought after, and got in readiness to send to the shore.
As so many officers were on board, these separate things each
might have had *one* to superintend their being collected; when
they might have been all got upon deck before the quantity of

water in the ship, afforded any interruption, or preventative. All these general necessaries might easily be sent to land upon the hawser; and would be instrumental in effecting great things, towards their final preservation. To the meanest capacity it must plainly appear, that by the instrumentality of the Floats and the Chaise Rolante, *every one on board the ship might have been safely landed.* And by securing to their use the necessaries specified— they would be enabled to coast it along to the Cape, or fall in with some vessel at sea. If the boats were not spacious enough to contain the whole company, provisions, &c.; another might very soon be constructed by the carpenter's and caulker's crews, with all their tools in their possession. During their voyage they could go ashore to refresh as they might find it necessary, and with the sails and cordage preserved, erect tents, not only for the accommodation of the females, but for the *comfort* of the whole company. By the life preserving apparatus, they would be able to land through a surf, (that would otherwise prevent,) by sending two or three men with Floats on, to the shore with the end of a hauling rope, by which they might assist the smallest boat to land in safety; the whole crew of this boat should then assist the next boat, and so on till all the boats were landed.

By the primary use of the Life Preserving Apparatus, and general application of the plan, I am fully persuaded it is more than probable, that the enormous sufferings and destruction which assailed the people belonging to this unfortunate ship might have been prevented; and *every one* of them finally *preserved!*

List of passengers who perished.

Col. and Mrs. James	Mrs. Logie
Capt. Waterhouse Adair	Mr. Newman
Col. D'Espinette	Miss Dennis
Capt. Talbot	Miss Wilmot
Mons. Oliver	Mr. Taylor
Mr. Hosea	Mr. Williams
Mrs. Hosea	John Sussman

Miss Hosea	Master Saunders	}
Master Law	Master Chambers	} Children

With several others.

I believe nine Europeans, seven Lascars, and two black women, were all that survived the distresses and ruin that followed in the train of this unfortunate and much to be regretted shipwreck.

HALSEWELL East Indiaman.—I think it very probable, that the night signals would have informed the people on shore, even while she was at anchor; and would have brought them to the cliff. On her striking, an immediate communication might have been opened: and *my mind* tells me, that the far greater part, if not the whole of those on board (not excepting the ladies,) might have been saved.

HERMACON.—This Brig ran ashore unexpectedly through the weather being thick. Although some habitations are not far from the spot, the people on the shore knew nothing of the wreck until after the crew had landed. From this vessel striking the ground so unexpectedly—exposed to heavy breakers, and beginning to creak and cry out in her timbers as though she would immediately go to pieces—and not a living creature to be seen on the shore to afford assistance; the crew were very reasonably seriously alarmed, and the younger part of them especially, being allured by the fine appearance of the sand (like unto the Anson's people) and trusting to their activity and to their skill in swimming, leaped overboard. Of these, only *two* got to land, and were afterwards very active in assisting to save those who had not been so *precipitate* as themselves, and were yet on board; but unfortunately in this ship-mate-like and humane work—they both fell a sacrifice to the *deceitfulness of the sand!* On her grounding, with the Apparatus on board, a man with a Float on, should have proceeded to the shore with a line, or a small hauling rope, as they were so close in.—He should then have slipped the Float off from himself, and fasten it to the rope so far from the end of it; as would admit

of the Float being hauled back to the wreck, while the end of the
rope remained with him. Another of the crew should then put on
the Float and leap overboard, when the first one would haul him
to land. Thus they might have proceeded until they were all saved,
and this they might have accomplished in a very short time. This
to me is as clear as the shining of the sun, and I presume must be
to every one.

HARPOONER.—This was a most melancholy wreck—
which when considered in its nature and issue—whole families de-
voured;—families divided;—some preserved, others lost;—will
appear as distressing as most upon record. Contemplate the fate
of the Wilsons, the Armstrongs, the Primes, &c.

While every feeling mind will lament the catastrophe, *much
consolation* is to be derived from the narrative;—inasmuch as it has
upon *the face of it indubitable proof*, of the *necessity* of *every ship
being furnished with the Apparatus*. Plain, *illustrative proof*,
where, and *how*, it might have afforded *preservation* to *all* who
perished; (those excepted who were drowned between decks, on
the first rushing in of the water,) and of course pleads in language
much more powerful than any I can use, for its adoption. The
greater part of the readers of this, by referring to the narrative of
the wreck, and consulting what I have already said of my Apparatus, and of its application, will readily discover how it might
have been applied in this case with efficacy; but because difficulty
shall not interrupt a clear conviction with any one, I will explain.

In the first place, let it be remembered, the Harpooner ran
on the rocks in the night. At the dawn of day, there was not a
living creature to be seen upon the shore; nor yet a habitation:
consequently the *preservation* of the people on board, depended
solely on the *means they themselves possessed*, and could reduce to
practice. The mate and four men, (at the risk of their lives,)
were fortunate enough to reach the shore in a boat; but it being

broken to pieces against the rocks in landing, could be rendered
no longer serviceable. It would have been a very reasonable measure, had the end of a line been sent to the shore by the boat: and
the omission, fully proves how the minds of persons encountering
the dangers of shipwreck are distracted. The situation of the poor
sufferers at this period, must have been truly distressing; for on
opening a communication with their comrades on the shore, solely
depended their safety. The sailors then ransacked *their* resources,
and "tried *many ways*, but they proved *all ineffectual.*" What
a picture of distress and misery must the crowded deck now
represent?!!

But at this joyful moment of anxiety, doubt and fear,—that
kind providence which so often interposes to succour distress
when at its height, interposed now; and "induced them to use
their *ship dog*," to do what their own skill and exertions had failed
to perform. By means of this valuable animal, a rope was got to
land, and a hawser strained, and fastened to the rocks: a sling
was also rigged for the people to sit in; with a block to run upon
the hawser, &c. No doubt, but this was as complete a machine, as
their means, and their perilous situation allowed them to construct.
But alas! (useful as it was,) it was incompetent to perform all
their work of preservation, in the space of time to which they were
limited! It must readily be supposed that these preserving means
(having no better,) were very acceptable: but a gentleman who was
saved "describes the mode of conveyance to shore as truly terrific"
it was with *difficulty* he was saved, and then "at the expence of
suffering many severe bruises."—several of those conveyed to land
were hurt and maimed." Lieut. Wilson fell a sacrifice to the *defectiveness* of the conveyance; and so did Mr. & Mrs. Armstrong,
their son and two daughters; "who could not be prevailed upon
to *attempt their passage to land*, by *means so exceedingly terrific!*"
Indeed it may be said, that the insecurity & general incompetency,
of the mode of conveyance to shore, was the cause of the whole
loss of lives: or in better words, had *One Chaise Rolante* only,

6

from my apparatus been on board, as an *assistant* to the means
they really made use of, it must be evident that *its* security and
competency would have SAVED THEM ALL! And first,—the
time which was expended in rigging the sling, would have been
saved, by the *immediate* application of the Chaise Rolante to the
hawser; by which several persons might have been safely conveyed to land, while the sling was *preparing*. The account says,
"about 6 o'clock of the 11th the first person landed, by means of
the rope;—about half-past one, 30 were saved by the rope. Here
then we are informed that 30 only were conveyed to land by this
means in seven hours and half: so that each averaged 15 minutes.
When I made my *first trial* of the Chaise Rolante, it occupied only
a little more than two minutes to convey a man across Porthleaven
Harbour and back again: nor was it tried *how soon* it could be
accomplished. (One of the spectators told me the time, I never
once thought of observing.) It is not improbable, but the distance
the Harpooner was from land, was less than across Porthleaven
Harbour; but admitting it to be equal, a question cannot exist
respecting the Chaise Rolante making *at least four turns* for *one* of
the sling; and children might have been taken in safety on a
grown person's lap. Hence it very clearly appears, that while the
174 that were saved, were conveying to the shore by the sling—if
the Chaise Rolante made only two turns and a quarter for one; a
number exceeding the *whole* who first embarked, might have been
landed, within the same space of time! Besides, my wheels would
not have injured the hawser by friction, so it would not have broke
so soon. But when the loss of time is calculated, that was occupied in making the many ineffectual attempts to get a rope ashore;
and that in which the dog was occupied in doing it; it must appear as clear as the light at noon-day, that *All* might have been
landed in *safety, several hours before the ship went to pieces;* provided the ship had been furnished with the apparatus.

HORATIO.—This was another melancholy wreck. Returning to their own port,—within a few hour's sail of it, the

accident was the more distressing. She stranded upon her own
soil, only a few yards from shore, where great numbers of friends
were assembled ; but alas ! only to be spectators of the melancholy
scene ; for assistance could not be communicated. Only *two* saved !
My apparatus being on board would have saved them all, with the
greatest ease ; this is plain ; read the narrative—it is a strong advocate for the adoption of my plan.

A Gentleman of Carnarvon was so kind as to write to me
on the subject of this wreck ; in his letter he says, " From the
above you will be able to conclude how far your apparatus would
have been useful, and how it should have been applied.   I readily
conceive had it been on board, every soul would have been saved :
among whom, were a very respectable gentleman and his lady,
passengers.   Vessels are very often stranded in Carnarvon Bay.
The 22nd last December, a Vessel was wrecked very near this
place ; she also was contiguous to the shore :—yet the crew were
all drowned, 12 in number !   Doubtless had your apparatus or
some other *been there*, they would have been all saved !   Last
month there were 3 vessels wrecked here, 1 ship (west indiaman,)
1 cutter, and 1 sloop—near 20 people were drowned !   It is very
probable *they also* might have been *saved* by the help of *your apparatus*.   I most sanguinely hope, that you may prosper, and that
your labours under the directions of the Lord, may be a means of
saving many from a watery grave."

JANE and REBECCA, Transport.—Is another spirited
advocate for the adoption of my apparatus and plan.   Every one
of the fine fellows lost here, might to a certainty have been landed
by *One Chaise Volante* with ease and safety, very many hours before the ship went to pieces.

JOHN and AGNES.—By the night signals, the people upon
shore might have been informed of her distress, and also the spot

on which she grounded : by which means the life-boat would have been enabled to rescue every one on board.

LITCHFIELD, 50 Guns.—Another melancholy wreck ; the narrative of which has many plain evidences upon the face of it, sufficient " to *convince the unconvinced,*" where and how the apparatus could have been applied, to have saved the whole of them who were drowned! Supposing there had not been any other part of the apparatus on board, but *one Chaise Rolante* to run upon the hawser (which by *their own* means they contrived to get strained from the wreck to the shore,) the extensive preservation it would have afforded (as in case of the Harpooner,) is too evident to need any explanation, Surely the fate of these hundreds of our fellow creatures and countrymen who were drowned, are now pleading and crying aloud for the adoption of the apparatus. Reader, refer to the narratives of those wrecks, and *you will join* me in my assertion.

LEONORA, French Vessel.—Might not the Apparatus have been used from the vessel, or from the pier, and have afforded preservation to the five poor fellows who were drowned ?—I am quite of opinion it might,—and would at the same time have rendered the risk the brave men in the pinnace ran, unnecessary.

PHŒNIX.—Affords proof of the advantages that would result from the use of the *Chaise Rolante.* We here see " there were sick and wounded, who could not avail themselves of the (coarse and dangerous) methods made use of to get ashore." And " some *died* of *the wounds* they *received* in getting ashore." If these instances of loss of lives, are not *evidences too plain to be mistaken,* in *favour of the plan* of preservation ; surely then, *judgment must fail in its office to discriminate.*

PHEATON.—This vessel was only about 50 yards from the shore, & stood upright five hours at least.—Read the narrative.

It plainly shews how the apparatus being on board, would have afforded preservation to all the crew and passengers. *This is quite clear.* If the projecting part of the apparatus *only* had been *present*, preservation might have been afforded to all on board ; for it appears, that *the sailors* hauled the boat to the wreck, after they had the end of a rope brought to them. But if the whole of the apparatus had been on board, to have been used in the early part of the disaster, it is more than probable that some of the portable valuables might have been preserved, as well as all their lives.

SCEPTRE.—The advantages which would have resulted in this case, from the apparatus having been on board, cannot be *ascertained ;* but may be *surmised.* The distance she grounded from the shore is not mentioned in the narrative : I have no doubt however upon my mind, but ropes might have been got to land, and the means contained in the apparatus made use of, to the preservation of most (if not all) of the people.

The idea very forcibly operates upon my mind, that *the ship itself might have been preserved!*—Many, at the first glance at this assertion, may probably start at the idea of such a large ship of war, being preserved by so small an apparatus. Read the narrative—" the launch was hoisted out with a view of getting the end of a cable from H. M. S. Jupiter ; she was however unfortunately upset and totally lost, together with her crew." Consequently this plan was frustrated, and the advantages which would have resulted, were not obtained. Now it may readily be concluded, that the officers of the Sceptre, conceived that the end of a cable being got on board from the Jupiter, would have afforded such assistance, as to prevent from driving on shore. From this expedient, *preservation* of the *ship was certainly calculated upon.* Unfortunately, they were not possessed of means to achieve this desirable object : but if my apparatus had been on board those ships, a line could have been projected from one to the other to a certainty : (there cannot exist a question on this head) then, by

the line, a rope might have been hauled; and by the rope, the
end of a cable might have been got on board: and thus, the
ship might have been preserved, and the 348 men, besides officers,
who perished with her! Should not then every ship be furnished
with the apparatus; seeing it is not possible to know, *when, where,*
or *how,* it may be rendered capable of, and wanted to afford
preservation?

SAN JUAN PRINCIPE, was a melancholy wreck, about
two thirds of the crew were drowned! As this ship came ashore
upon a fine beach, I cannot see why, *all* might not have been
saved. The process would have been nearly the same as described
for the Anson. The narrative does not give the circumstance attending her coming ashore; but supposing there was not any person on the beach (to lay hold of a line if one was projected) then,
an active man with a float on, should have gone ashore as described
in the Grosvenor's case. That this could have been accomplished
is clear, from the circumstance of the poor sufferers " floating upon
pieces of the wreck towards land; " affording proof that the current was setting towards the shore. The whole of the people belonging to this unfortunate ship might thus have been saved. I see
no room even for a doubt to arise respecting it.

TROIS AMIS, the whole of the crew might have been
saved.

TWO FRIENDS, Transport, speaks loudly for the adoption of the apparatus. Owing, only to a concurrence of providen-
tial circumstances in their favour, and all on board must have
perished! It was high water when she struck; she must have
been a very strong vessel; and the surf could not have been heavy,
or she would have gone to pieces long before the people were
landed; 36 hours at least having elapsed before that was effected.
Look at the narrative, and the advantages the apparatus would
have afforded, are very discoverable.

In the foregoing instances, the utility of the apparatus has been applied to cases only of common shipwreck,—of vessels stranded; but its means of affording preservation are not confined within such a narrow compass; they are not limited to accidents occurring on the shore, but extend to the wide Atlantic, or any other part of the great deep. As vessels are liable to casualties, far at sea, as well as near the land, upon sands, or upon rocks; the benefits which will arise out of the apparatus being on board every ship, are incalculable; because every case to which it may be applied, cannot be even *conjectured*. However, many cases can be enumerated, wherein very desirable assistance, and extensive preservation may be afforded.

It is not an uncommon thing to see accounts of vessels *upset*, *water-logged*, and *foundering* at sea;—of vessels being distressed for want of provisions, and from other causes. Now, whether poor mariners are perishing from one cause or another; among rocks, or in the midst of the sea; they are perishing: and have an equal claim upon humanity for assistance: this is a truth that nobody will attempt to deny. But, *humanity* in the greater number of desperate cases at sea, have not in time past been able to afford assistance; no more than in general case of shipwreck upon shore. "The weather was too severe, we could not board." "The sea was running so high we could not approach," or such like, have frequently been the concluding sentence to a sad tale, of one vessel having fallen in with another in distress. I hope, however, the efficacy of my apparatus, for the future will obviate such difficulties. I have never heard of any means devised, or scheme proposed, for affording assistance and preservation at sea; or that it were even thought on, until it was strongly suggested to my mind, that the properties of my own invented apparatus, might be applied to those purposes: and I may of a truth assert, that I have now made it such, as to be highly calculated for, & adequate to afford every *possible* assistance, and preservation, in the general course of casualties to which mariners are exposed; *any where,* either abroad or at home : in the midst of the great deep,—as well as in the midst of a foaming surf : and almost under any circumstance, or in any situation.

The promptitude, precision, and facility being so evident, with which a communication may be opened, by my methods of conveying a rope, I do not think it necessary to say much in argument to produce conviction, of the apparatus possessing the means to do what I have been alluding ;—but believe that elucidating by the introduction of a few cases, will furnish abundance of convictions, both of its capacities, and of its value.

INVINCIBLE, 74 Guns.—Read the narrative, and it will plainly appear, how the means of communicating ropes, and use of floats, might have afforded very extensive preservation. Upwards of 400 poor creatures found a watery grave : and I am very sanguine of belief that the greater part, or even *all* of them might have been saved ! After the Collier joined, the floats might have been put to work, and kept going, (even after day light had disappeared,) as long as was necessary.

JUNO.—With the wreck of this ship, the Brig Jessia fell in, and on it found one man, who had been in that distressing situation three days. Capt. Williams kept by the wreck four hours *waiting for a favourable period* in the weather to send his boat to the poor fellow's rescue.

In this case, three things are very conspicuous; the very distressing situation of the man : the christian patience of Capt. W. in waiting so long by the wreck : and the signal interposition of divine providence in preserving the man in the midst of such immediate peril—in directing the Jessia to the very spot—and in lulling the wind and soothing the sea to enable Capt. W. to take him off the wreck ! Much might be said on this subject,—but I leave it for the feeling mind to contemplate ; and shall briefly ob-

serve, that *with my apparatus on board*, Capt. W. could with ease
have conveyed a Float to the man, and have got him safely on
board his vessel in a few minutes. *This is clear :* and it is as clear
also, that had the Jessia, a Commander *less humane* than Capt. W.
the man would have been left to perish ! "The weather would not
permit coming near the wreck" or some such like *plausible* reason
would have presented itself to the minds of men, not so sympathetic as Capt. W. and would have furnished sufficient excuse for
passing on, like the priest and the levite in the parable : but Capt.
W. acted the part of the good samaritan ;—and for such an act is
entitled to the thanks and esteem of every good man.

HIBERNIA,—"The Lord Nelson, Barton, from Demarara, on the 31 March, 1816, Latitude 41. Long. 39. spoke the
Hibernia, from Demarara to Belfast, in want of provisions ; but
blowing hard, could not board her : her bottom was foul and she
sailed heavy." Now, with my apparatus on board, a rope might
have been conveyed from one to the other ; and by it a cask of
provisions, or any other thing, easily transmitted. As it was, "not
being able to board," (it is very probable it was the case, I do not
mean to question it,) the poor fellows' distress was not relieved.
Thus they were fallen in with, a long way from port, *in want of
food ;—in want they were left ;*—and for aught I know,—*through
want they perished!*

DUKE of CLARENCE, Capt. Lowry, February, 1816, on
her passage to Lisbon, from Falmouth ; fell in with a Prussian
Ship, name unknown, from Corunna to Bilboa, in the bay, on her
beam ends, in a sinking state : her crew were on the wreck. The
Duke of Clarence immediately hoisted out her boat, and succeeded
in getting seven from the wreck. In a second attempt, the boat
(which was proceeding with the mate and one of the men belonging to the Prussian Ship also in it,) filled, before they could reach
the wreck ; when both these poor fellows who had just been taken
from the wreck, were unfortunately drowned. The Clarence

H

could render no farther assistance on account of the inclemency of
the weather." So the remaining poor fellows on the wreck, were
left to their fate!—to perish! As the ship was in a sinking state
when discovered, of course she soon went down; and ended the
misery of those on board, whose state of mind must have been
agony itself, rendered excessive by the *preservation* which had just
been *along-side*, but had not stretched out its *life-giving* hand to
them! Surely the meanest capacity must instantly discover *what*,
by the apparatus being on board the Clarence, could have been
done :—how easily a line might have been projected, and a Float
or two conveyed to the poor perishing men upon the wreck, and
the whole of them saved; without risking one of their own people,
or taking the trouble to hoist out their boat. The business is *so*
plain, to comment would be waste of time ;—"would be burning
day light." Does not this *one circumstance*, utter language stronger
than the finest oratory of man, for the adoption of my plan? Does
it not utter *volumes* of *imperious pleadings* for every ship to carry
the apparatus?! By doing which it is probable, *hundreds of lives*
will be saved every year *at sea!*

        I had nearly forgotten to mention, that I requested a friend
at Falmouth, to call on Captain Lowry, and to describe to him my
method of conveying a rope to a distance, my Cork Floats, &c.—
and to ask if he had been furnished with such things, could not he
have rescued the men who were left upon the wreck. Capt. Lowry
replied, " If he had such *instruments*, he could have saved all their
lives : and thought the invention a very valuable one."

        The means comprised in the Apparatus, may be yet extend-
ed, to a variety of important purposes at sea. It is not an uncommon thing I presume for vessels in company, or when they meet,
to communicate with each other : and for a vessel that has received
injury by severe weather, to communicate her situation and wishes
to a consort, (especially on the approach of night,) may be of the
utmost importance. A ship having been long from home, might

wish to know *News*, or might have *Letters* to send, &c. Now, in any of these cases, when the state of the weather prevents nearing each other, and prevents communicating in the usual way;—by means of the projecting line, &c. the difficulty may readily be obviated.

To the Commander of a Fleet,—for such purposes, the Apparatus must be of infinite value; as probably dispatches he might wish to send off immediately, might be delayed a considerabe time, through *not being able to board.* I believe an obstruction of this kind, retarded information of the interesting battle, off Trafalgar ; for Lord Collingwood in his letter says, "having blown a gale of wind ever since the action, I have not yet had it in my power to collect any reports from the ships." In this case, a line might be projected from one ship to another, and *all the reports collected :* this might be safely done through the medium of my WATER PROOF TRANSIT ; and finally, if the weather continued boisterous, the dispatches might be transmitted by the same means from the commander's ship, to the one intended to carry them, and be forwarded without any let or hindrance.

His Lordship also says, (in letter of 24th) "In my letter of the 22nd, I detailed to you for the information of my Lords Commissioners of the Admiralty, the proceedings of His Majesty's Squadron on the day of action ; since which I have had a *continued series of misfortunes :* but they are of a kind, that human prudence could not possibly provide against, or my skill prevent. On the 22nd a strong southerly wind blew with squally weather, which did not, however, prevent the activity of the officers and seamen of such ships as were manageable, from getting hold of many of the prizes, (13 or 14,) and towing them to the westward, &c. &c.—— On the 23rd the gale increased, and the sea ran so high, that many of them broke the tow-rope, & drifted *far to leeward, before they were got hold of again :* and some of them taking *advantage of the dark* and boisterous night, *got before the wind,* and have *perhaps*

H 2

drifted upon the shore and sunk." Now it must be very clear to every one, that by each of the ships having my Apparatus *on board*, a great deal of excessive labour might have been saved, and difficulty obviated; and consequent upon this,—those ships which "took advantage of the darkness of the night to run away", might have been saved also: for, by my method of throwing a line, the *tow-ropes might speedily have been re-placed:* this is clear: and thus those parts of the fruits of the hard-earned victory, (which through these accidents were lost,) might have been *preserved!!*— Under a variety of circumstances at sea, the getting a *tow-rope* from one vessel to another, may be of serious importance.

In case a Fleet at Anchor should be assailed by a storm; the end of a cable being conveyed from a ship dragging her an- chors, to another riding comfortably on safe ground, might afford preservation by preventing her from driving ashore. The narra- tive of the Sceptre elucidates this. On the 14th January, 1812, a large convoy experienced a heavy gale of wind, while at anchor in Falmouth Harbour.—Before day light, the Queen, Transport, from Lisbon, with invalid troops and their families on board, par- ted her cable, and before another could be got out, she struck on Trefusis Point. And in 20 minutes after, she became a complete wreck.—Out of 330 persons on board, 230 perished! among the number were several officers and their wives. If my Apparatus had been on board the Queen, I think assistance might have been afforded, by means of a rope being conveyed to the nearest ship, when the Queen was drifting. At any rate it might have rendered extensive preservation after her going ashore; there cannot be a question about this.

PILOT BOATS, frequently find it both very difficult and dangerous to come along-side; and though a distressed ship may be perishing for want of assistance, yet, it may not be afforded through "not being able to board."—With the apparatus on board, the transition of a Pilot might be safely effected. Communication being so easily opened by a rope, while at a safe distance; a Pilot-Boat might be hauled along-side, either to windward or leeward, or under the stern. But if severity of weather prevented all approach, then by the use of the *Float* the pilot might easily be got on board in a few minutes; suffering the only inconvenience of being wetted.— Pilot Boats should certainly be furnished with a small sett of the Apparatus; it would be frequently found beneficial to return to port: for after having gone to sea, the surf may increase very much, so as to endanger their safety, if not insure their destruction by attempting to push through it. *Safety* would be very much promoted by the assistance of a few men on the shore hauling on a rope communicated from a boat: this would keep her, *end on,* and excessively facilitate her coming in. See the advantages of this method, at the close of the narrative of the Ingebord Yacht.

The Boat recorded Page 23, to have been lost near Gorleston, might have been preserved by the means recommended; for the danger attending on her coming in, was very apparent; and was conversed on, by those in the boat, and some persons who were on the pier-head : if then the end of a rope had been conveyed from the boat to those on the shore, there cannot be a question but she might have been brought through the surf, and her crew preserved!

His Majesty's Ships or others, may be urgent to *land a boat,* when much surf on the shore prevents, or renders it highly dangerous; but by the boat having *the line projecting part* of the Apparatus, would be able easily to accomplish what would otherwise be insurmountable. For, while without the breakers, a rope might be conveyed to the people on the shore, by whose assistance a landing would be easily accomplished. If *Dispatches* or *Letters only,* were wanted to be landed; this might be done by the water proof transit in a few minutes : the boat remaining without the breakers.

I apprehend that instances occur of men falling over board while vessels are under way, when projecting a line to them might be instrumental to save their lives. Or boats upsetting in harbour when passing from one ship to another, might have had assistance afforded, if the ships were furnished with the apparatus. I beg to introduce the following instance. Dock Telegraph, Oct. 5th, 1816. " During the gale of saturday last, a boat with a seaman belonging to one of the Portsmouth Vessels, upset off mount wise; the unfortunate man struggled a few minutes with the waves and endeavoured to reach an oar which was thrown to him from a Schooner anchored near the spot, but his strength being exhausted he sunk in the sight of several agonized spectators." Now, by " an oar being thrown towards the man from a schooner," proves that he was *near* by; consequently, had the schooner the Apparatus on board, a rope might have been conveyed to him before the boat upset, which would have saved him and the boat also. But I have a method for projecting a line from *a man's hand*, to relieve such like distress as the above related ; and I am of opinion that the man might have had the line conveyed to him from the schooner in two minutes (at most,) after the boat upset ; consequently he would then have been saved.

I conceive that projecting a rope from a vessel about to go into a Pier in rough weather, would afford important assistance.

Might not the Apparatus be rendered highly beneficial in case of Fire at Sea, when it would be dangerous for vessels or even boats to go very near ?—*I think* it might be rendered excessively useful to assist the people on board, to escape.

Having shewn (I trust to the satisfaction of my readers,) how my apparatus may be made instrumental to preserve vast numbers of human lives from premature destruction, it may be imagined that conviction of its value will be general ; and that *all* will eagerly sanction and urge its adoption.

I am certainly very sanguine of belief, that *most* will thus feel, and perhaps *do*, as far as *their power* may enable them ;—that *every* impartial and dispassionate person will thus decide: but as the minds of men are liable to be prepossessed, I cannot expect thus much from *all*, until prejudice is subdued. If prejudice does not exist against my apparatus, I know it does (or did) exist (in some instance, but perhaps in a circumscribed degree,) in favour of another, which has within these few years past been introduced, "for saving persons from vessels stranded on a lee shore." It is very probable, however, that this prejudice is *now* much diminished ; as *experience* has fully *proved*, that IT *does not possess efficacy*. It will readily be understood, the apparatus alluded to, is Capt. Manby's : and be it as fully understood, that it is my sincere intention, while necessity obliges me to speak of it, to do it with the most scrupulous respect. But, in *Justice* to my own invention, and more especially in justice to the cause of *Humanity*, I shall feel impelled to speak the *truth* unreservedly. *More* than the truth, I am not aware that I have spoken, while setting forth the properties of my own apparatus ; I am not aware that I have exaggerated. This I know, & now affirm, that I have not advanced any thing contrary to my clear opinion and belief; nor *will I*, while speaking of Captain Manby's.

It is true, that while pursuing my own subject, I heard of Capt. Manby's method of throwing a rope from the shore, to a stranded vessel ; but I did not once think that it (any thing like,) comprehended what I had in view ; or that it would interfere with what I was contriving : because, (as I have already said,) from the first, I intended my Apparatus to be used on ship board ; and Capt. Manby's is constructed to be used only on shore.

I thus went on upon the plan that my own ideas furnished; and beg leave to assert, that I have not borrowed a single particle from any apparatus, to compose my own. On the contrary, when a gentleman of this town, offered me the perusal of a book, which treated on Capt. Manby's apparatus (it may be 18 or 20 months since) I declined it, because my invention should not be influenced, either directly or indirectly, by any thing resembling it :—that it should be original.

With these intentions, and in the manner stated, I pursued my plan; and about the end of July, 1815, had made such progress, as induced me to make application to a gentleman in London, for his advice and patronage. This I did, and received a very handsome and kind reply : The following is a part of its contents, dated August 6th, 1815. "It will give me much pleasure to assist in bringing forward any plan which has for its object, the saving of seamen's lives.—You are publicly aware that Capt. Manby's Apparatus for throwing ropes to vessels in distress, by means of small mortars, are about to be sent into all the maritime districts. I think you should not proceed to London at this season of the year, &c." I conceived the meaning of this last clause, "not proceed to London, &c. to signify, "being on the approach of winter, it may interrupt Capt. M's plan, and thereby prevent some lives from being saved, which otherwise would be, by its instrumentality." As this did not alter my opinion respecting the evident difference between Capt. M's plan and my own, I took the liberty to reply, to the following effect.

I beg to return thanks for your kind letter, which I received to day. Since my last, I have laid my plan before a Lieut. of the Navy, who highly approves of it ; and thinks my method for projecting a rope, superior to any other yet devised : particularly because of its portability, and ease of management. And he highly approves of my idea, for every ship to be furnished with the apparatus,—when it would always be at hand, wherever the use of it might be necessary.

" A few days only have elapsed since I heard of " Capt. M's Apparatus being about to be sent to all the maritime districts," and I respectfully beg to suggest, that it should stimulate me to bring forward my plan immediately;—because, if *mine* is *preferable*, the trouble and expense of sending *such a vast number of mortars, as will be necessary for all our coasts,* may be saved; and so little labour is requisite in the construction of my Apparatus,— it may be brought into use this approaching winter.

Not wishing in the least to detract from Capt. M's plan, the Lieutenant above spoken of, thinks *it cannot be efficient* on our coast, because of the *impossibility* of having it on all occasions on the spot when wanted; and many melancholy instances have occurred, where a few minutes lapse of time only, have caused the loss of many lives. In addition to the method of throwing a rope, my machine for conveying persons or property to the shore, meets the Lieutenant's highest approbation," &c.

To these observations I received a reply about the 27th, in substance as the former, with the addition " that Capt. Manby's apparatus was actually in a state of preparation to be sent to the places appointed; having been sanctioned by Government."

I was previously ignorant of these things;— the information however altered not my convictions, but I of course with-held from advancing any thing further on the subject, and waited in silence to see what *proofs* the winter would afford, that Captain Manby's *Apparatus* and *Plan* possessed such extensive life-preserving means, as to render *any other unnecessary.*

During the winter, several vessels were wrecked in this district; and no assistance afforded by any apparatus. Wrecks happened on various parts of the coast, in most of the maritime districts, within the United Kingdoms; and no mention of lives being saved by the apparatus. There was one instance indeed, (and *only one* that came under my observation,) wherein the crew of a vessel, was preserved by it, and she ran on a flat sand, (I do

I

not recollect where,) and kept together a considerable time. I do not assert that this *one* instance, was the *only one* wherein Captain Manby's Apparatus afforded preservation; but it was the only one the newspapers presented to my notice; although through the same medium, I read of many shipwrecks. Nor was I at that period induced to make memorandums of what I saw narrated relative to wrecks, as I have done the last winter; therefore, have it not in my power, to make particular statements. Some of the wrecks, however, were attended with such great loss of lives, as coul not fail to arrest the attention, and concern, of every person possessed of feeling.

In January, 1816, Three Transports were wrecked on the coast of Ireland, with the immense loss of *Six Hundred* of our fellow creatures! our countrymen,—our friends; (the greater part of them, brave fellows returned from the murderous day of Waterloo,) here—in one common ruin—met a hasty—a premature destruction.

To look no further into the list of shipwrecks that occurred during the winter, *this* great loss of lives, surely afforded a *very sufficient proof*, that Capt. Manby's Apparatus was *defective* either in *itself*, or in its *use*; and of course, afforded also a *very sufficient excitement*, to *supply* deficiencies; and to amend, and to improve. The ensuing summer *afforded* the *opportunity* of *doing this*; and it may reasonably be conjectured, that *every possible* thing, *was done*, against the return of winter. As the value of human life is *too* great to be *trifled* with; too important, for its preservation to be *neglected*; it would be uncharitable to suppose that those who had the superintendant management of the plan altogether, had *overlooked* the *necessity* of *giving*, or had *neglected to give* it, *all the efficacy* it were *capable* of *receiving*.

The winter again in course of revolving time returned, and brought with it, its usual casualties; and after having committed excessive ravages upon our shores, have once more left us, with a swollen catalogue of shipwrecks!

Now, it will reasonably be allowed that in proportion to the number of shipwrecks,—so *opportunity* for assisting and relieving distressed mariners presents itself. Opportunities then have been very abundant this last winter; but (strange as it may appear) I have not seen a single instance recorded in the newspapers* where Capt. Manby's apparatus has been rendered useful to save life! From the numerous accounts of shipwrecks which have come under my observation in the course of the winter, I have noted down no less than TEN VESSELS *lost upon our own shores*, and ALL THEIR CREWS PERISHED!! At several other wrecks, destruction made great ravages;---of those on board one ship, only the carpenter saved; another ship, only one passenger saved! two other vessels lost, and only three saved out of their numerous crews, &c. &c.

Were I to express the ideas that present themselves on viewing this part of the subject,—perhaps, I might be censured by those who are prepossessed, for being a partial judge; and for delineating with a *self-interested* pencil; I therefore desist, and beg that my readers will view and contemplate the subject for themselves. Surely it is so manifest that "he who runs, may read;" and, "so plain, that a way-faring man cannot err."

However, I conceive I may be permitted to observe (without passing the bounds of candour,) that so many wrecks, attended

---

* I regularly read the Evening Courier, and Bell's Weekly Messenger; and during the last Winter Months have not neglected the opportunity of reading more than Five or Six Papers. I generally look over our Two Provincial Papers; and very frequently the Dock Telegraph. I mention the papers I usually peruse, that my readers may have the opportunity of correcting me, if I have been guilty of over-sight.

with such extensive loss of lives, carry strong evidences with them, that Capt. Manby's Apparatus *does not possess the power* of affording general preservation to shipwrecked persons. And, if the apparatus were capable of *possibly receiving* that power, not a doubt can exist, but it would have been *given* to it *long ago*. For Capt. Manby has had at *command every means* and opportunity, both *internally* and *externally*, of giving his plan every possible efficacy, & of *proving its merits*. As then the *proofs* are *wanting*, agreeable to the nature of things it must follow, that the *power to afford them does not exist*. If it does exist, *why has not preservation been afforded*, in so many recent melancholy instances, wherein it was claimed by perishing men?! The Question must answer itself.

As I have freely expressed my belief, that the *inefficacy* of Capt. Manby's Apparatus must be *self-evident* to every considerate person; so I should think, *from whence* the inefficacy proceeds, must be *as evident*. I will now introduce the substance of a letter I addressed to Isaac Head, Esq. (Collector of the Port of Gweek,) which will partially exhibit what my ideas were *then*, respecting it; and also further illustrate.

Helston, September, 1816.

To ISAAC HEAD, Esq.

Sir,

As by your request I looked at Capt. Manby's Apparatus, while it lay at the Custom House, so I have this week looked over the explanatory printed sheet; and while I see much to approve, the inefficacy of the plan is very visible. As the description of any thing cannot convey ideas, or enable one to form an opinion equal to an inspection of the thing itself; I shall draw my conclusions chiefly from what I saw at the Custom House. I saw a Mortar on its bed, a Hand-barrow, and a large coil of rope; (there were besides, several large Casks, Boxes, &c. not open,) and which on viewing. I was led to decide with you, and others who saw them; that although they may be made useful in certain cases, they cannot *possibly* be applied generally. Indeed, reflection must inform any one, that two men carrying an *unloaded* hand-barrow, from place to place along our coast in winter, would find it difficult to proceed; as many of the paths and places through which they would have to go, are generally by the rains, rendered almost impassable for persons empty handed: how then can a load of some hundreds weight be transported, and where hedges too, frequently interfere? The *impossibility* is so evident, to enlarge would be waste of time. But Sir, supposing it could be removed from place to place, with any *tolerable conveniency*,—then, the *time requisite* to bring it to the spot where wanted, would to a *certainty*, insure the destruction of the persons, it were intended to preserve.

Capt. Manby himself says, " Vessels frequently go to pieces very soon after taking the ground," and *we know* that vessels wrecked on our coast, frequently go to pieces *directly*. Whence then the *possibility* of saving the lives of those persons on board such vessels, *by any means*, which would require some hours to be brought to the spot? In reviewing the nature of our coast, and the nature of the apparatus—it appears certain, that the advantages it is capable of affording must be very few: this Sir, you and all our neighbours must know. In the nature of things it must be so —it cannot be otherwise.

Within the few years last past, several vessels have been lost in Porthleaven Bay, and you know that in many cases, if a man had been dispatched *to the Depot*, on the swiftest race-horse, the instant these vessels grounded,—to fetch the apparatus; and could he bring it all in *his pocket*, you know he would not have been back in time, to have saved the lives that were lost! instance the Brig at Porthleaven, last December twelve months, when half the crew perished: and the Wine Vessel at the Loe Bar, when 9 out of 11 were drowned! Both these vessels went to pieces *di-*

rectly, and supposing that any Life-Preserving Apparatus had been
even within a mile, at the moment they took the ground ; where
was the *possibility*, of its being brought *in time*, to afford preservation to the crews ? Possibility was as distant as the east from
the west,—this is self-evident. For as the vessels went to pieces
directly, preserving means must have been upon the spot at the
moment, to be rendered useful ; and if providently they had been
there, *all the poor sufferers* might have been saved !

Far, very far, be it from me to detract from Capt. Manby's
invention ; speaking the truth on so important a subject, can never
be detraction. When the safety of multitudes of our fellow creatures is at stake, to *with-hold* any truth would certainly be sinfully
culpable ; and additionally so, when " *England expects every man
to do his duty*." I believe I have said no more than any impartial person will say. Your old friend Lieutenant King declared
that for miles in the neighbourhood of his residence, if a vessel
came ashore in a storm ; a life-preserving apparatus could be useful only, by being upon the spot. Mr. Hall, Comptroller of the
Customs at Scilly, informed me, that the Collector and Custom
House Officers had decided on the inefficacy of Captain Manby's
Apparatus : and were he enquired of by His Majesty's Ministers,
he should reply to the same effect.

We see then that Capt. Manby's Apparatus, although having the means within itself of affording assistance to shipwrecked
mariners *when circumstances will admit*, cannot possibly afford
assistance *generally*, and indeed *only very partially*. Nor is it
possible for *any Apparatus* (however extensive its powers, or portable in its construction) to be rendered generally useful on shore.
Vessels must be furnished with the means on board, or their inhabitants can never calculate upon having preservation afforded to
them, in case of being wrecked through stress of weather : to this,
all I have conversed with on the subject, do readily assent.

By a vessel having a sett of my apparatus on board as a part of
her equipment, the means of preservation would be at hand in whatever part of the globe, accident might occur: and the knowledge
of having those means in possession, would greatly tend to keep
the minds of the distressed *undisturbed,*—which of itself would be a
great assistant to their preservation. We read in an account of
the wreck of a Transport, "*seeing no prospect of being saved,*
many went below, and with their friends *yielded* themselves up to
their fate." Here—and at the melancholy wrecks on the Norfolk
coast, the 1st and 2nd lust. (where whole crews were drowned,)
might not my apparatus have been instrumental in saving many
lives? surely it might. Then Sir, as a friend to humanity, do urge
its general adoption. Besides, the expense is a mere trifle, as a
very few pounds, (in proportion to the size of the ship,) will provide a sett. Moreover, a plan I have (if adopted,) will exempt
Government from any (or scarce any) standing expense. At the
same time, I do not wish for the disuse of Captain Manby's; my
object is to do good—to preserve life. Captain Manby's Apparatus has been instrumental of saving lives—at which I rejoice: but
yet we have *to lament an extensive loss;* there is yet room for any
preservative to be employed—and I am certain that mine is such a
one, as will call forth general approbation."

I hope the following extract of a letter I addressed to the
printer of Bell's Weekly Messenger, the beginning of Oct. 1816,
(but which was not published till some time in November,) will
not be thought superfluous after the preceding; as it was followed
by a letter from Doctor Muter, containing many very pertinent
remarks on Capt. Manby's Apparatus, part of which I intend
also to subjoin.

Extract from my own letter.

"Capt. Manby's Apparatus (to be used from the shore in
case of shipwreck) comprehends purposes and means, that mine

does not : and my Apparatus comprehends things, purposes, and means, that Capt. Manby's does not ; and is peculiarly calculated for, and is intended to become, a necessary part of every ship's equipment ; for in it are comprised the means of affording assistance and preservation at sea, as well as when wrecked on the shore : and which from its portability and simplicity, can almost under any circumstance be made use of.

The advantage of a ship having such an apparatus *on board*, must be apparent to the meanest capacity ; as it would *always* be at hand, *whenever*, or *wherever* it might be wanted.   That I entertain an opinion of my invention possessing *superior* means ; and that it is calculated to afford *superior preservation* ;—is a fact.   Yet, while with humble confidence I thus express myself, I do not intend, or even wish to depreciate the worth of any other ; but common sense will tell every one, that only a *very small proportion* of wrecked vessels, can *possibly* be made to partake of the benefits attached to *any* life preserving apparatus that is kept on, and used from the shore :   and in this opinion, am not I supported by the issues of the numerous shipwrecks in the late gales ? "

A few weeks after the publication of my letter, there appeared a letter dated Battle, December 17th, 1815, signed Robert Mater, M. D. from which I take the following.

"Remarks on Capt. Manby's Plan for conveying a line from a lee shore, to a vessel stranded on the coast.

THE PLAN is too limited in design, being confined to the coasts of Great Britain and Ireland.   Shipwreck is a casualty, that should be calculated upon as possible to befall every vessel at sea.   Why therefore, should we confine our solicitude for the safety of our mariners to our own coast ? It is wrong in principle ; the line should not be conveyed from the coast to the stranded vessel, but from the vessel to the coast.—It is difficult to be executed.

DELAY. It would be *impossible* by *any effort* to convey his apparatus from the place in which it may be kept, to any considerable distance on the adjacent coast, in so short a time as always to meet the instantaneous emergency of shipwreck.

DARKNESS presents another, and occasionally, an insuperable obstacle; unless there should be a light on board the wreck, it may be so dark, that the vessel cannot be seen.

To make many remarks now is unnecessary, as in the preceding pages several applicable ones may be found. I have already expressed my opinion on the superior precision, with which a line may be projected by my method; and which, for the purposes at sea I have mentioned, must be of great advantage : but to open a communication from a stranded vessel with the shore, precision is not necessary, as, if the line reaches the shore any where, it can hardly be wrong. Another advantage attending my plan is, that a far greater length of line may be projected by the same portion of impulsion ; for in proportion as the wind may be violent, so will it afford assistance ; while on the contrary it will afford proportionate opposition to a line projected from the shore. It cannot but be evident that the same projectile, whatever it may be, will go to a far greater distance before the wind, than against it; perhaps nearly double in a storm, which is a matter of importance.

"The obstacle which darkness presents, and which is occasionally insuperable," has no interference with my means, and plan of using them from the vessel. First, as before stated, precision is not necessary ; those on board cannot easily err in the direction : secondly, the light of the rocket will insure the immediate finding of the line. I purpose also an improvement on the common rocket, that on discharging itself, it shall take fire and burn for several minutes. By this method I conceive there will be no "difficulty of execution," or time lost in groping for the line after it reaches the shore. The eligibility of a rocket, must be apparent to every one

K

who knows what a rocket is. It has my unbounded good opinion—
and had from the very first; although I did not know how to use
it with certainty for so many years: here I encountered great difficulty, but happily it is at last conquered. I do not know Doctor
Muter's method of using a rocket; but the testimony he bears to
the promptitude with which *it may be used*, and the distance it
may be thrown,—is gratifying.

When I looked at Capt. Manby's printed sheet, by Mr.
Head's request, (twelve months ago) on seeing that the plan altogether was so widely different to my own, I was not very particular
in reading the " *Observations, &c.*" but before I conclude (having
already 70 pages out of the press) I have borrowed the sheet to
peruse it more minutely, and although I again discover the very
great difference in our plans,—yet I find that many of our ideas
on the subject of them, are in unison.

It is very true that "no branch of the service demands more
nicety, than the mode of laying the *rope* in readiness to be carried
out by the shot." And I conceive the faking or laying of it in the
basket, to be as perfect a method as can possibly be devised. I do
not question but the same method answers very well for the log-line
also; but I believe that my method is yet more simple, and requires
less room for stowage. When I first began to project a line, I
bought some in balls, which was wound up very nicely as *tea twine*
and *packthread;* and very similar to balls of cotton, that ladies
use for sewing. It immediately struck me, that I could not arrange
it any better, as I found it would run out very freely from the
inside. On making my experiment, I fixed the internal end to the
rocket, and laid the ball on the ground unconfined by any thing.
On discharging the rocket, the line went out with the most possible freedom; the ball on the ground being scarcely agitated. The
method highly pleased me, but then I could not tell how to put
the line into a ball again: here I was perplexed, as I conceived
that to put up the line as it came from the manufacturer, a machine

was necessary. I then tried other methods, but none of them being satisfactory, I had recourse to my balls again; and after much enquiry found that the only *machine* used (for such size line as mine) is a wood pin, round which it is wound in a spiral direction by the right hand, while by the left it is held, and kept almost constantly turning round. After a little practice I learnt to do it very well; and 1 feel conviction that there is not any method in *the whole world*, by which more line can be stowed away in the same compass, or admit of its running out with more freedom. I feel additional satisfaction in finding it is a method of all others so well adapted to my purpose, as I have learnt that sailors are well acquainted with it. Last summer, I projected some lines before two naval officers; and on their observing my manner of putting the line into ball again, one of them laid hold of a line, and presently put it into a ball round his thumb; saying that sailors were used to such work, as they always *balled their yarn* in the same manner.

From Bell's Messenger of October 7th, 1816, I copied the following:—"By the port letters it appears that considerable damage has been done to the shipping on the coast by the late gales. In one instance the crew and passengers of a wrecked vessel, were saved by a life-boat sent from the shore. These life-boats ought to be provided in every creek and harbour along our shores, for the deliverance of shipwrecked mariners."

From Capt. Manby's Sheet now before me 1 transcribe as follows:—"From a consideration of its vast importance, I have devoted much of my attention to produce boats, calculated in any weather to rescue lives and property from wrecked vessels. The boat generally called the Life-Boat, though admirably calculated for particular services, is so large and cumbrous, that it is at times very difficult to convey it to the point of danger, &c. These and other causes have not only thrown it into disuse, but have produced such a neglect of it, that, in some places, I found it in a

state of decay. I am therefore induced to submit the simplest and
least expensive mode, that has suggested itself, to me, of giving to
boats of whatever size and construction the principle of the life-
boat. The plan is to place an empty cask (of eight or ten gallons
measure, securely bunged and perfectly staunch) beneath each
thwart in an upright position, and secure it by two pins on each
side, and the properties of a life-boat are given to the most common boat in use. If the boat thus fitted, should fill, no more is
necessary than to pull the plug out, and the boat, rising from its
less specific gravity, will let all the water through at the plug-hole."
Now, by this plan suggested by Capt. M. "every creek and harbour
may be provided with life-boats;"—and as it is so cheap and so
simple, any one who possesses a boat, may easily give to it these
good properties. Those accustomed to go to sea in rough weather
in the common sort of boat, who know of this method and refrain
from its use, obstinately expose themselves to dangers they might
avoid. By a boat having such buoyancy given to her, as to prevent her sinking, those who compose her crew, would have confidence and courage to push out to sea in such weather, as would
otherwise overawe them :—hence extra good might be done.

About a week since I had an opportunity of reading an
account of a pilot-boat belonging to Scilly, that went off to a
vessel in distress; when suddenly she upset, and seven out of fifteen that composed her crew, were drowned; leaving five widows
and fifteen children to lament their loss. Now, had this boat the
life-boat properties given to her, might not this loss of life, and
consequent distresses upon surviving relatives and friends, have
been prevented? I am firmly of opinion, if the buoyancy recommended is generally given to boats (especially to pilot-boats) that
much good will ensue; both in preserving their own crews, and
by enabling them to extend their efforts to preserve others : and it
is from this belief, and supposing that my pamphlet may fall into
the hands of many who reside on the coast, and are not acquainted
with Capt. M's plan, that I have inserted it. And I do hope that

such of them as are accustomed to encounter tempestuous seas, will immediately make the addition to their boats, which may be so easily done; and which, while it is every way so highly calculated to promote their own advantages, will enable them to extend their services to their fellow creatures in distress.—I should not omit to insert for guidance in regulating the buoyancy of boats, that "two gallons of air are enough to support a man's body." It is not my intention, however, to particularize on Capt. M's plan; yet, (although I have adverted to the inadequacy of it, to accomplish its own intention) I should consider myself to be wanting in duty to the cause I am striving to serve, and in justice to Capt. M. were I silent on that part of it that is so congenial to my own ideas, and that commands my warmest approbation. I do not know that I should have made a single observation on its defectiveness, only through compulsion. But to combat and refute the arguments and objections that have been started, or that may be started to oppose the adoption of my life-preserving means, because "Capt. Manby is *on the ground before me*"—and "his Apparatus is sent into all the maritime districts," I have been laid under absolute necessity, to point out its inefficacy; and the *impossibility* of rendering *it*, or *any other* apparatus generally useful, that is kept upon land. I trust I have afforded convincing proof of this to every one; and also that in doing it, I have not passed the bounds of candour: I am not conscious that I have,—I hope I have not:—I intend only to make plain, simple statements. I hope also that Capt. M. himself will give me credit for my intentions; and as our objects are so near of kin, that his liberality of mind will lead to assist in promoting the adoption of my plan; and the sooner, as there is not a single article belonging to it, that is similar to his own, (at least I do not know that there is). As I purpose that my Apparatus will shortly be in London, to prove the fate that awaits it. No doubt but Capt. M. will have an opportunity of passing his opinion on it;—at any rate he will do it JUSTICE; this I have a right to claim from ALL, and I expect no more from ANY.

It is true that during the long period I have had the plan in hand, it has cost me much in thought, time, labour, and expense; but I am not so anxious for remuneration as I am for its adoption; being fully satisfied that its utility will soon be proved, and that if I am rewarded in proportion to its value, it will be even beyond my wishes. I do not know that any further remarks at present are necessary: and all that I now solicit is,—that my Invention and Plan may meet with serious and impartial consideration.

POSTSCRIPT.

The following observations did not present themselves to my mind in time to be introduced in their proper places, or else they were overlooked till too late. I therefore think it will not be deemed improper, to introduce them now.

From Capt. Campbell's Shipwreck ; and which should have appeared on the 16th page, to have elucidated the certain destruction, attendant upon the mind being so unhinged :—"Out of eleven Europeans and fifty-six Lascars on board, only Capt. Campbell and Mr. Hall (two passengers) of the former, and four-teen of the latter were saved from the wreck ; the rest having been drowned in attempting to save themselves; excepting some, who overcome with terror, anguish, and anxiety, and exhausted with fatigue, had bid a formal adieu to their companions, let go their hold, and calmly and voluntarily gave themselves up to the deep." Now it must be observed, that this wreck was very close to the shore, and yet more than three-fourths of the people were drowned! It is an instance that clearly exemplifies how the "auxiliary destroyers" consume more of life in many cases, than. wreck itself. It is also an incontestible illustration of what I have advanced on the 32d page.

On Saturday last (9th August) I saw a farmer who resides near to the spot where the JANE and REBECCA was wrecked, and who was among the first to go under cliff, to assist in getting the people ashore. I conversed with him on the subject, and showed him my Apparatus; all of which he highly approved, and said if they had a *Chaise Rolante*, they could easily have landed 100 men, more in the same space of time: consequently (as I have said on, the 49th page) every life would have been preserved; and a great deal of property (consisting of dollars, &c.) might have been sayed also.

I beg to call particular attention to the following. In course of applying the use of my apparatus to the shipwrecked vessels in the narratives, I have omitted the RESOLUTION. According to the view that I have of things, I consider it as more than probable, that the apparatus having been on board, would have been instrumental to *have preserved the vessel and her cargo!!* Indeed, I calculate upon this to a pretty great certainty. Refer to the narrative;---it is there said that the anxiety of the crew to insure a chance for their preservation, induced them to cut their cable, and ran ashore just as the tide had begun to ebb. I do not know that any person has blamed them for it. Perhaps it was a justifiable act,—a prudent measure; for they had an opportunity of beholding the heavy breakers upon the shore, and of calculating upon the almost certain destruction that would assail them, if they should be forced amongst them upon a flowing tide. But provided they had my apparatus on board, they would have known, that if they should be stranded at *any period* of the tide, they had something to trust in for deliverance. They would have known, they had the means of sending a line to the people upon the shore, even before the vessel touched the ground, and the means calculated to remove them in a few minutes from their distressing situation to the shore in safety. *Knowing this,* they would have felt confidence in running the risk of their cable holding, and have let it hold as long as it would; in hopes that the weather might abate, or the wind might shift, &c. and that thereby they might be enabled to save their vessel.

To have ran the risk, a fine moon-light would have been an additional incentive; the moon was only one day past full, consequently moon-light throughout the night. Well then, let us now look for the issue that might have been expected. In less than two hours after this vessel came ashore, to the destruction of so much property; the wind eased, and also shifted to a point quite favourable for her to have gone round the Lizard : the weather also cleared at the same period, and it was as bright a moon-light night as we had for the winter. Now, had the crew the life preserving means on board, to have inspired them with confidence to run the risk, and (says one of the Porthleaven pilots) " had her cable held for that short period only, she might then have cut her cable to advantage,----have flapped her wings, and soon have turned her back upon Porthleaven."

Under such circumstances then, it must be evident that the Apparatus may even become instrumental in affording preservation to ships and cargoes ; for it is a well known truth, that many cables have been cut, and running ashore at a favourable period of the tide has been had recourse to, as the only probable means distressed mariners had to use, to *insure even a chance* of preserving themselves.

Trathan, Printer, Falmouth.

NARRATIVES of SHIPWRECKS.

<hr>

AMICUS, from Petersburgh, Captain Simpson, Commander.--Though we cannot give the particulars of the commencement of this unfortunate event as fully as we wish; yet the subsequent preservation (of a part) of the crew, and the heroism of the spectators, as prompted by humanity, will it is presumed, render this narrative extremely interesting.

At 4 o'clock on Tuesday morning December 8th, 1807, in a tremendous gale of wind, with a heavy snow, this ship laden with hemp, tallow, &c. struck on the Holderness Coast, half mile south of the Sister Churches. At 12 o'clock, the Captain who was an excellent swimmer, committed himself to the waves, with a rope, hoping to be able to gain the shore, but was overwhelmed by the breakers, and perished in the attempt. The Mate and another of the crew followed his example, and met with a similar fate. The remaining part of the ship's company were seen clinging to the rigging and wreck, by numerous spectators.

After several ineffectual attempts to assist these unhappy sufferers, Mr. Giles had recourse to the following: he procured a leaden half-pound weight, and making a hole through it, he fastened it to a long piece of whip-cord, and selected from the spectators the most athletic man, to cast it at the wreck. After many fruitless trials, the man, following a receding wave, succeeded in throwing it across the vessel. The Carpenter fastening the cord round

B

his arm, was dragged through the surf to the shore, apparently
lifeless; but he afterwards recovered. The cord was again cast,
and a boy was rescued from the vessel in the same manner.

After this, a person named John Greensides, notwithstanding the heavy surf, rushed through it to the vessel ; and though he
was hidden repeatedly by tremendous waves, and could not swim,
he succeeded in gaining the wreck, and brought to land another
boy. In his passage to the shore he was twice thrown down by
the violence of the back water. He again returned to the wreck,
and at the hazard of his own life, saved the life of another seaman.
At six o'clock, four persons ventured through the waves to the ship,
and brought away two others, who died shortly after their gaining
the shore. The bodies of the captain and mate were afterwards
washed on shore.

The ACTIVE, Thomas, from Limerick to Bristol, was
totally lost, 20th February, 1817, with all her crew; near the
mouth of the River Cushin, Ireland.

BOADICEA—(With the Sea Horse and Lord Melville,) in
January, 1816, sailed from Ramsgate, with Troops on board;
bound to Cork in Ireland. She encountered blowing and thick
weather, and arrived off the coast of Ireland, and not being able to
weather some head lands, came to an anchor in (I believe) Court
Mashery Bay ; blowing a hard gale of wind and heavy sea running.
At night she had a light at her mast head—which about midnight
disappeared. In the morning her fragments were discovered among
the rocks which lie between the two strands of Garrett's Town,
and where she had been driven after parting from her anchors in
the night. Near to the wreck was a rock somewhat elevated
above the surface of the water, and upon it were seen 80 or 90
persons who had scrambled thither from the vessel.

The people from the shore communicated to them as well
as they could, that the only chance of safety was for them to re-
main there till low water. This reasonable advice however, was
unheeded by a great part of them : their situation was so excessively distressing as to overcome their rational faculties ; in it, they

were perishing from wet and cold—they could endure it no longer, and in attempting to come ashore near 30 perished! About
50 who remained upon the rock till the tide ebbed, were saved.
Out of 280 who were on board this unfortunate ship,—220 were
lost.

The Ship BARBADOES, Capt. Parry, belonging to Liverpool, was lost on 10th October, 1816, on the rocks of Scilly,
coming from Smyrna with a valuable cargo. The Captain and 15
men took to two boats, which were soon upset and all perished!
The chief-mate Mr. C. Grumly, the only one saved, says that he
was the only one left on board when the boats quitted the wreck;
that he constructed a raft on which he put himself, and was driven
to sea; was picked up two days afterwards by a small French
vessel—and landed in France.

BLUE BONNET, of Stanrain, Bevan, was totally lost
near Gervan, the 20th Jan. 1817, when all on board perished!
The fragments of this vessel were discovered scattered about in the
morning.—It was supposed by the situation of her bottom among
the rocks, that she grounded about two or three in the morning,
upon the top of the tide—only about 50 yards from the shore.
The dead bodies of the crew were found upon the shore, inter-
mixed with the wreck.

The CONSTANT, Alves, from the Brazils to Bordeaux
was totally lost, the middle of February, 1817, on the rocks of
Corduan.—Only two seamen saved.

CHASSE MAREE, laden with wine, totally lost on
Charmouth Beach, about 20th January, 1817,—with *all the crew:*
Cargo saved.

DROITS DE L'HOMME, 74 Guns, (having troops on
board) made the whole of the people on board her to amount
to the great number of 1750.—I expect this number does not in-
clude English prisoners who were on board, comprising 3 infantry
officers, 2 captains of merchantmen, 2 women, and 48 seamen
and soldiers, making 55 souls. " About 4 o'clock in the morning
of the 14th January, 1807, this ship went ashore in Hodierne

B 2

Bay—shrieks of horror and dismay were heard from all quarters,
while the merciless waves tore from the wreck many early victims.
Day-light appeared, and we beheld the shore lined with people
who could render us no assistance. At low water, rafts were constructed, and the boats were got in readiness to be hoisted out.
The dusk arrived, and an awful night ensued. The dawn of the
second day brought with it still severer miseries than the first, for
the wants of nature could scarcely be endured any longer, having
been already near 30 hours without any means of subsistence, and
no possibility of procuring it.   At low water a small boat was
hoisted out, and an English Captain and eight sailors succeeded in
getting to the shore.   Elated at the success of those men, all
thought their deliverance at hand, and many launched out on their
rafts; but, alas!—death soon ended their hopes.

      Another night renewed our afflictions. The morning of the
third, fraught with still greater evils, appeared ; our continued
sufferings made us exert the last effort, and we English prisoners,
tried every means to save as many of our fellow-creatures as lay in
our power.   Larger rafts were constructed, and the largest boat
was got over the side.   The first consideration was to lay the surviving wounded, the women, and helpless men in the boat; but
the idea of *equality* so fatally promulgated among the French, destroyed all subordination, and nearly 120 having jumped into the
boat in defiance of their officers, sunk her. The most dreadful sea
I ever saw, seemed at that moment to aggravate the calamity;
nothing of the boat was seen for a quarter of an hour, when the
bodies floated in all directions: then appeared in all their horrors,
the wreck, the shores, the dying and the drowned ! Indefatigable
in acts of humanity, an adjutant-general, Renier, launched himself into the sea, to obtain succours from the shore, and perished in
the attempt.

      Nearly one half of the people had already perished, when
the horrors of the fourth night, renewed our miseries—weak, distracted, and destitute of every thing, we envied the fate of those
whose lifeless corpses no longer wanted sustenance. The sense of

hunger was already lost, but a parching thirst consumed our vitals. . Recourse was had to urine and salt water, .which only in: creased the want : half a hogshead of vinegar indeed floated up, of which each had half a wine glass ; it afforded a momentary relief, yet soon left us again in the same state of dreadful thirst. Almost at the last gasp, every one was dying with misery, and the ship, which was now one third shattered away from the stern, scarcely afforded a grasp to hold by, to the exhausted and helpless survivors.

The fourth day brought with it a more serene sky, and the sea seemed to subside ; but to behold from fore to aft, the dying in all directions, was a sight too shocking for the human mind to endure. Almost lost to a sense of humanity, we no longer looked with pity on those whom we considered only as the forerunners of our own speedy fate, and a consultation took place to sacrifice some one to be food for the remainder. The die was going to be cast, when the welcome sight of a man of war brig renewed our hopes. A cutter speedily followed, and both anchored at a short distance from the wreck. They then sent their boats to us, and by means of large rafts, about one hundred (out of four hundred who attempted it) were saved by the brig that evening. Three hundred and eighty were left to endure another night's misery, when, dreadful to relate, above one half were found dead the next morning

I was saved about 10 o'clock on the morning of the 18th, with my two brother officers, the captain of the ship, and General Humbert. They treated us with great humanity on board the cutter, giving us a little weak brandy and water every five or six minutes, and after that a basin of good soup. I fell on the locker in a kind of trance for near thirty hours, and swelled to such a degree, as to require medical aid to restore my decayed faculties. We arrived at Plymouth on the 7th of March following. To that Providence, whose great workings I have experienced in this most awful trial of human afflictions, be ever offered the tribute of my praise and thanksgivings !

Elias Pipon, Lieut. 63rd Regt."

The DIAMOND was lost August 31st, 1816, near Cape Romaine Shoals, having on board officers and men about 50. The Schooner Hornet, witnessed the melancholy catastrophe and tried to get alongside, but after many *ineffectual attempts* and loss of anchors and cables, was compelled to give it up. The crew then finding they were left to shift for themselves, constructed a raft on which they got, on the ship going to pieces—soon after, one of the men (the survivor who narrated this melancholy tale) was washed off—and seeing one of the hatches of the ship near him, succeeded to get upon it, on whioh he floated till picked up by a vessel,—it was supposed that all the others upon the raft perished!

DANISH SHIP.—Extreme Distress Relieved.—On the 25th March, (or April,) 1806, His Majesty's Ship Orpheus, was cruising off the coast of Norway; which in the mildest season of the year is noted for the dreariness of its climate and the tempestuous seas that surround it. We observed a Danish Ship, at the distance of a few miles, to he in an instant upset, and completely buried from the view of those, who but a moment before had distinctly seen her. Our Captain (who is humanity itself,) instantly ordered the ship to be wore towards her, and though we were ourselves in a hazardous situation, not many miles from a coast, with a furious gale blowing directly for the shore. As we approached towards the vessel, we observed her to be in a truly deplorable situation, with her bottom nearly upwards; whilst the poor fellows on board were clinging to the part out of the water, and occasionally waving their hats to entreat our assistance.

We had now prepared a boat, intending to veer it empty towards her, and stood as close to her as possible, consistent with our own safety: but had the mortification to find, that to render the poor fellows on board any assistance, was utterly impossible. From the tremendous sea that was running, had the two ships by any accident been brought into contact with each other, it must have been attended with inevitable destruction for both. There was therefore nothing to be done, however painful the consideration, but to leave these unfortunate people to their fate, and to

seize the first favourable opportunity, (if they should be fortunate
enough to survive,) of administering to their safety. Of this hope
we were not destitute, from the buoyancy of her cargo, consisting
of timber, and through the vessel having righted, through the loss
of her masts, and otherwise much shattered.

But if *our* feelings suffered so much at being thus compelled to let the dictates of humanity, give way to those of imperious
necessity; it may be easy to imagine (tho' hard to describe) what
must have been the sensations of those unfortunate wretches, whom
we observed wringing their hands in all the agony of despair, some
mounted in the rigging of the remaining masts, and in the most
earnest manner, entreating our assistance : while the sea with ra-
ging fury, assailed the vessel in all directions, and threatened to
overwhelm them with instant destruction.—The darkness of the
stormy night, now shrouded them from our view, and brought
with it to all of us, I believe, sensations, not of the most pleasant
nature.—The gale continued with unabated fury, until the morning of the second day following, when it gradually subsided into a
calm. This operated greatly against our purpose, as we were now,
according to calculation, fifteen leagues asunder. We continued
to make what progress we could. On the fifth day at 10 A. M. we
again discovered the wreck, and in an instant every possible sail
was set. About noon we succeeded in bringing off these poor
wretches, to the number of nine, only one of the crew having been
drowned by the accident. They were pale, emaciated, and reduced to the last degree, and so benumbed with cold, as to be
completely helpless.

During the five days, they had no sustenance whatever, except, what they providentially derived from a fall of snow on the
third day. We had them carried down to our mess-room, and
seated round a fire. They were then, by direction of the surgeon,
plentifully supplied with warm tea and bread and butter, not
thinking it prudent after so long fasting to allow them food of a
grosser quality. Our next attention was directed to their cloathing,
and our Captain ordered them to be cloathed with a warm and

complete suit each. They were then stripped, and their legs and feet bathed in warm water : and some of our honest seamen, (notwithstanding the bleak state of the weather,) very chearfully resigned to each of them a bed and hammock. On the next day the limbs of some of them exhibited symptoms of mortification ; but from the care and attention of the surgeon, the circulation was gradually restored, and in a few days, we had the satisfaction to see them completely restored : and that they were not deficient in gratitude to their benefactors. Our relief towards those poor fellows was well timed, and even perhaps in a few hours might have come too late ; as in a short time it came on to blow hard, and the vessel was at the time of our meeting with her, nearly gone to pieces, and only three leagues from a dangerous reef, so far detached from shore, as to preclude every possibility of assistance from thence. This therefore may be considered as a signal instance of the intervention of divine providence ; and affords us the important lesson, that amidst the most imminent peril, we ought never to despair ; but confidently to rely on the protection of him who ruleth the earth."

I have been particular to insert at length the foregoing narrative—which was transcribed from a letter written by an officer on board the Orpheus ; because it admirably depicts the character of Humanity : which in a general sense, is so well supported by British Seamen. And another reason for inserting it so fully, is to set forth the propriety of continued exertions in the work of humanity,—seeing how well the crew of the Orpheus were re-paid for their labours. I presume the *satisfaction*, resulting from having afforded preservation to so many fellow creatures must have been far more abundant than the richest ship as a prize, could possibly supply.

It furnishes also a proof (among the many to stimulate us) that "*we should not be weary in well doing*." And it reduces to practice the Golden Rule, which our Lord enforces—"As ye would that men should do unto *you*; do ye even so *unto them*."

And if my maritime readers, on perusing this narrative, are possessed by the same feeling that pervade my breast, while using my pen ; whenever opportunity presents itself, *they will* "*go and do likewise.*"

DISPATCH.—This vessel having on board, part of Gen. Sir Hussey Vivian's own Regt. and Lord George Cavendish, a son of the Earl of Waldgrave, and other officers returning from the Peninsula; was unfortunately wrecked off Coverack (10 or 12 miles from Helston) in February 1809. I believe she had a very favourable passage home, and made the Lizard in tolerably good weather; but not being able to reach Falmouth Harbour by day light, it was deemed most prudent to lay to till morning, as the night was very dark. All hands being pleased with the thoughts of being so near home, and with the expectation of being safe in harbour in a few hours, made themselves comfortable; the captain supped with the military officers, &c. Unfortunately, gladness supplanted prudence; the deck was neglected, and of course the duties of the night. The sailors being lulled in the arms of ideal security, had forgotten to calculate upon the course and power of the current, which runs very rapid along this part of the coast, (and I have been informed by a gentleman of Falmouth, that at one particular spot, it makes towards the shore, whether the tide is ebbing or flowing,) and which about one o'clock in the morning carried them upon the rocks: and as the wind had risen during the night, and made a considerable surf upon the shore, she soon went to pieces; when melancholy to tell, only five were saved out of all on board! These could scarcely tell how they escaped, other than that they were thrown by the waves upon the rocks, and were fortunate enough to scramble their way up the cliff. Many others were also thrown in upon the rocks, but through the darkness and want of assistance, they fell victims to the fury of the surf.

It was a remarkable circumstance, that about the same hour of this disaster, the PRIMROSE Sloop of War, outward bound, was lost upon the Manacles : only one boy was saved, who was found a day or two after, floating on a part of the wreck.

DOVE of Dartmouth, Williams Master, laden with Culm; on the 1st July 1817, encountered a hard gale of wind; and having

c

her boom carried away, and received other damage, was prevented from working round the Lizard. She then made a tack to the westward, but soon found she was falling to leeward, and that there was no probability of being able to fetch Penzance; so let go two anchors in Porthleaven Bay, and brought up off *the long sand.*

She rode pretty well considering the wind and sea she was exposed to, but unfortunately after a short space, the anchor to which her best cable was bent, broke; when directly after, her other cable parted, and necessity obliged her going ashore. The Captain being well acquainted with the coast, wished to run into Portjew, or Gunwallo Church Cove, (which lay a little to the eastward, having a flat shore with a fine firm bottom;) but he could not from the damage his vessel had received, work far enough to windward, so was obliged to run on the east end of the long sand, (nominated Gunwallo Fishing Cove,) in the midst of very heavy breakers. She immediately broached to, and the beach being stiff, she rolled several times most frightfully, which rendered the situation of the four poor fellows, who comprised her crew, truly distressing. The tide, however, having ebbed about an hour, allowed the country people the opportunity of going upon the sand, to render every possible assistance; which they could not do at high water, as at that period, the waves ran boldly up to the cliff.

The people of the neighbourhood who exerted themselves to assist the crew, being aware of the dangerous nature of the sand, used the precaution of putting a rope round the waists of those who volunteered themselves to encounter the surf, the end of which was held by their comrades. Thus they were enabled to approach the wreck so near, as to throw a fishing line on board, which was laid hold on by the master, who put it round his arm. At this moment, *a smooth* * presenting a fine opportunity, and the vessel being heeled inwards, one of the men (an experienced sailor, and

---

* A smooth (so called) is when the sea abates its fury for a short space, and for a few waves does not break so heavy, nor run so far in upon the shore.

a thoughtful, intelligent man,) jumped from the vessel upon the sand; and fortunately, not falling off his feet, he immediately made all the haste he could to get out of the reach of the sea; and he succeeded to admiration, without the water once impeding him: his escape was indeed wonderful.

The captain was not so fortunate, though he jumped upon the sand just at the same moment the man did; for he fell off his feet, (which the man observed, but did not dare to stop to assist him, knowing that he had not a moment to spare, to escape himself from the danger which was so close at his heels,) and before he could recover himself, he was surrounded by the waves; and the line which was round his arm having got entangled in the wreck, his situation became perilous; when William Triggs, (son of Mr. Robert Triggs, of Mullion,) rushed into the surf, and succeeded in seizing him by the sleeve of his coat. They were both now off their feet, and beat and tossed by the surf; and the people who had hold of the end of the rope which was about Trigg's waist, being eager to get them both to land, hauled on it rather violently, when the captain's coat rent, and the piece came off in Trigg's hand, and he was dragged in without the captain; but another lusty young farmer, (called John Courtis,) observing the mishap, made a dash into the water, and being assisted, succeeded in bringing him to shore in safety. The other two poor fellows, from the period that going ashore was apprehended, had their spirits weighed down, and were overcome with dismay. One of them, (a young man about 18,) also jumped overboard, and soon found himself enveloped by the surf; which baffled his intentions, and

as before. The smooth here spoken of was extraordinary in its extent, and had much the appearance of being directed by a particular providence; for the sailor who embraced the opportunity which it afforded to escape, had scarcely his foot wetted in his passage from the wreck: and yet she was frequently deluged, both before and after, by the tremendous breakers, which very soon beat in her deck, and also a great part of her side, although she was a strong vessel. The ebbing of the tide prevented her being broken entirely to pieces. As it was she became a complete wreck.

increased his terrors. He then laid hold of a rope which hung over
the side, but could not regain the deck; and the waves continuing.
to pour over him, he soon disappeared.

The other man got into the weather shrouds, thinking the
mast would presently go by the board, and fall inwards, when he.
should go with it towards the shore; but he was either beat from
his situation by the heavy breakers, or else he let go his hold,
through being overcome with terrors, (which is the most probable,)
and fell into the water without the vessel.

Thus one half of the crew perished, in about ten minutes
after the vessel struck; notwithstanding she was only a very few
yards, from a number of the country people, who were present
when she grounded!

ENDEAVOUR, Stephenson, in attempting to go into
the Port of Whitby, 20th March, 1817, struck on the bar, and
went to pieces: all the crew perished.

FANNY, of Irvine, was totally lost, 20th March, 1817,
on Hoyle Bank: all the crew perished.

GROSVENOR, Indiaman, wrecked 4th August, 1782, on
the coast of Caffraria—being within a cable's length of the shore,
all hopes of saving her were at an end.

It is not in the power of language to describe the state of
distraction, to which every one on board, particularly the passengers, were at this time reduced. Despair was painted on every
countenance; mothers were crying and lamenting over their children; husbands over both; and all was anarchy and confusion.
Those who were most composed, were employed in devising methods to gain the shore. As one of the most probable, they set
about framing a raft; and it was hoped that by this means the
women, children, and sick would be safely conveyed to land. In
the mean time three men attempted to swim to shore with the deep
sea line; two of them succeeded; the other perished in the attempt. By means of this small line, a much larger was conveyed
to the shore; and by it, a hawser. In drawing the latter ashore
the two men were assisted by a great number of the natives who

were come down to the water's edge to behold the uncommon
sight: when the hawser was hauled on shore, it was fastened
round the rocks, and the other end made fast to the capstan on
board the ship, by which means it was made taught.

The raft being about this time completed, was launched
overboard, and four men got upon it to assist the ladies in getting
from the ship; but they had scarcely taken their station, before
the hawser which was fastened round it, snapped in two, and the
raft driving on shore, was upset; by which accident, three out of
the four men were drowned. In this dilemma, every one began to
think of the best means of saving himself. It should have been
observed, that the yawl and jolly-boat before this were hoisted
out, with a view to be applied in saving the crew; but these were
no sooner over the side of the ship, than they were dashed to
pieces by the surf: so that the only means of preservation, which
now appeared for getting ashore, was by the hawser made fast to
the rocks, hand over hand. Several got safe to land in this manner, while others, to the number of fifteen, perished in the difficult attempt.

The ship soon parted before the main mast. The wind providentially at the same time shifted, and blew right upon the land:
a circumstance, that contributed greatly towards saving those who
still remained on board, who had all got upon the poop, as being
nearest to land. The wind and surges now impelling them, that
part of the wreck on which the people were, rent asunder fore
and aft, the deck splitting in two. In this distressful moment they
crowded upon the starboard quarter, which soon floated into shoal
water; the other parts of the wreck breaking off those heavy seas,
which otherwise would have ingulphed them, or dashed them to
pieces. Through *this fortunate incident*, every soul on board, even
the ladies and children, got safe on shore; excepting the cook's
mate, who being drunk, would not be prevailed upon to leave
the wreck.

The second day after landing, was employed in collecting
together all the articles that might be useful in their journey to the

Cape, to which they very imprudently had resolved to walk; a resolution which involved them in complicated misery, and which cannot be justified by any wise principle. With materials from the wreck, they might easily have built a vessel capable of containing them all, as was done by Capt. Wilson, of the Antelope Packet. And particularly so, as the carpenter and caulker's crews all got safe ashore. They might then have coasted it along shore, putting into every bay as they proceeded, in order to water and refresh. They would thus have found a much easier and quicker passage to the Cape, than by attempting as they did to travel by land, subject to a thousand difficulties, the slightest of which were much too arduous and fatiguing for delicate women and children to encounter. *Distress, however, sometimes deprives men of all presence of mind;* so the crew of the Grosvenor.

HOPE, Allen, lost at the mouth of the Eyder, crew drowned. Lloyd's list, 21st March, 1817.

HALSEWELL, East Indiaman, wrecked off Seacombe, in the Isle of Purbeck, Dorsetshire, January 6th, 1786, was for two or three days beating about in the Channel; she encountered blowing weather, and received much damage. January 5th, at eleven P. M. they saw St. Alban's Head, a mile and half to leeward, upon which they took in sail immediately, and let go the small bower anchor, which brought up the ship at a whole cable; and she rode for about an hour, and then drove. They now let go the sheet anchor, and wore away a whole cable; the ship rode about two hours longer, when she drove again. In this situation the captain sent for Mr. H. Meriton, the chief officer, and asked his opinion concerning the probability of saving their lives. He replied with equal candour and calmness, that he apprehended there was very little hope, as they were then driving fast on the shore, and might expect every moment to strike. It was agreed, that the boats could not then be of any use.

About two in the morning of Friday the 6th, the ship still driving, and approaching the shore very fast, the same officer went into the cuddy, where the captain then was. Capt. P. expressed extreme anxiety for the preservation of his beloved daughters, and earnestly asked Mr. M. if he could *devise* any means of saving them. The latter expressed his fears, that it would be impossible; adding, that their only chance would be to wait for the morning, upon which the captain lifted up his hand in silent distress. At this moment the ship struck with such violence, as to dash the heads of those who were standing in the cuddy, against the deck above them; and the fatal blow was accompanied by a shriek of horror, which burst at the same instant from every quarter of the ship. The ship continued to beat upon the rock, and soon bilged, falling with her broadside to the shore. At this critical juncture, Mr. Meriton offered his unhappy companions the best advice that could possibly be given; recommending that they should all repair to that side of the ship, that lay lowest upon the rocks, and take the opportunities that might present themselves, of escaping singly to the shore. He then returned to the round-house, where all the passengers, and most of the officers were assembled: the latter were employed in consoling the unfortunate ladies; and with unparalleled magnanimity, suffering their compassion for the amiable companions of their misfortune, to overcome the sense of their own danger, and the dread of almost inevitable destruction. At this moment, what must have been the feelings of a father,—of such a father as Capt. Pierce!! The ship had struck on the rocks, near Seacombe; on this part of the shore the cliff is of immense height, and runs almost perpendicularly. The sea now broke in at the fore part of the ship, and reached as far as the main mast. Capt. P. and Mr. Rogers (the third mate,) then went together to the stern gallery, when after viewing the rocks, the captain asked Mr. Rogers if he thought there was any possibility of saving the girls. He replied, he feared not; for they could discover nothing but the black surface of the perpendicular rock, and not the cavern which afforded shelter to those who had escaped. They then returned to the round-house, where Capt. P. again seated himself between his two daughters, struggling to suppress the parental tear which then started into his eye. The sea com-

tinuing to break in very fast, Mr. Rogers made his way to the
poop; he had scarcely reached it, when a heavy sea breaking over
the wreck, the round-house gave way, and they heard the ladies
shriek at the intervals, as if water had reached them; the noise of
the sea at other times drowning their voices. Some part of the
wreck was still discernible, and the officers upon the rocks, cheered
themselves in this dreary situation, with the hope that it would
hold together till day-light. Amidst their own misfortunes, the
sufferings of the females filled their minds with the acutest anguish;
every returning wave increased their apprehensions, for the safety
of their amiable and helpless companions.

But alas! too soon were these apprehensions realized! A
few minutes after Mr. Rogers had gained the rock, a general shriek,
in which the voice of female distress was lamentably distinguishable,
announced the dreadful catastrophe! In a few moments all was
hushed, excepting the warring winds, and the dashing waves. The
wreck was whelmed in the bosom of the deep, and not an atom of
it ever discovered. Thus perished the Halsewell—and with her,
worth, honour, skill, beauty, and accomplishment!

This stroke was a dreadful aggravation of woe, to the
trembling and scarcely half-saved wretches, who were clinging to
the rocks, and about the sides of the horrid cavern. They felt for
themselves; but they wept for wives, parents, fathers, brothers,
sisters—perhaps lovers! all cut off from their dearest, fondest
hopes! 74 were saved out of rather more than 240.

HERMACON, French Brig, totally wrecked in the morning about sun rise, January 23rd, 1817, at the east end of the Loe
Bar of sand, in Mount's Bay; 9 out of 17 drowned.

HARPOONER, sailed from Quebeck 27th October 1816,
with about 400 troops on board, bound for London. About nine at
night on the 10th November, in thick weather she struck on the
outer rocks of St. Shots, Newfoundland. A great number of passengers were drowned on the first rushing in of the water before
they could get upon deck. The night was spent in miserable
suspense, not knowing their exact situation, and the ship thumping.

hard upon the rocks. The boats were washed off the deck, but the one hanging at the stern remained ; and at day-light the mate and four sailors volunteered, at the hazard of their lives to attempt to get ashore, with a view of getting some assistance : after severe struggling they obtained a landing, but their boat was dashed in pieces against the rocks ; and not being able to obtain any assist- ance, they went opposite to the ship and hailed to send a rope ashore. After trying *many ineffectual* ways, PROVIDENCE at last induced them to tie a small rope round the body of a Newfoundland dog, which they threw overboard. The dog immediately made for the shore, but was prevented from landing five different times, by the surf drawing him back ; but by the great exertions of the sailors on the rocks, the dog was got on shore, just as he was on the point of sinking. The master of the ship on board, made a large rope fast to the small one, which was hauled to land by the mate and the four men. They then rigged a sling to sit in, with a block to run upon the large rope ; by which means, all those saved were hauled to shore. Out of those saved are a Mrs. Wilson and daughter, (Mr. W. and three children drowned,) Capt. and Mrs. Prime were saved, (lost all their children,) Miss Armstrong saved —but her father, mother, brother, and two sisters lost! From the commencement of the disaster, death stared every one in the face—the hope of any individual being saved was very slight. It is impossible to describe the sensations which were excited at seeing the faithful dog struggling with the waves, and reaching the summit of the rock, dashed back again into the sea by the angry surf, until at length he arrived with the line. About six o'clock of the 11th, the first person landed by means of the rope,—during the passage to the sling, it was with the utmost difficulty that the un- fortunate sufferers could maintain their hold, as the sea beat over them. Some were dragged to the shore in a state of insensibility. Lieut. Wilson was lost from being unable to hold on the rope with his hands ; he was twice struck with the sea—fell backwards out of the sling, and after swimming for a considerable time among the floating wreck, (from which at last he received a blow in the

D

head,) perished! Many who threw themselves overboard, trusting
their safety to their swimming, were lost; they were dashed to
pieces by the surf against the rocks, and by the floating pieces of
the wreck.   About half past one o'clock 30 were saved by the
rope, several of whom were hurt and maimed.   The rope by constant work, and swinging across the sharp rock, was cut in two.
From that hour, (there being no means of replacing the rope,)
the spectacle became more than ever terrific—the sea beating over
the wreck with great violence, washed many overboard.   Their
heart-rending cries and lamentations, were such as cannot be expressed; families—fathers, mothers, and children clinging together!
The wreck breaking up, precipitated all on it into one common
destruction! Under these melancholy circumstances, 206 souls
perished! And the survivors have to lament the loss of beloved
relatives and friends.

    After the foregoing account was published in the Evening
Courier—in the same paper of 23d Dec. the following appeared:—

    A Gentleman who was saved and is arrived in England,
relates that 174 in all were saved. He describes the mode of conveyance to the shore as *truly terrific*.   He was immersed three
times in the waves; the last of which, (he also quite alive to his
situation) let go his hold from exhaustion; but being then close
to the rocks adjoining the shore, he fortunately escaped, though
at the expence of suffering many severe bruises.

    HORATIO, Capt. Hanny, from Trinidad to Liverpool,
was totally wrecked on Wednesday, at Dinas Dinble, in Carnarvon
Bay, only 2 out of 26 people on board were saved. A Gentleman
residing near the spot where this melancholy catastrophe occurred,
wrote to me the particulars: the following is the substance.

    The Horatio, from Trinidad to Liverpool, came ashore
about five o'clock in the morning, on a fine sandy beach: and
while the stiffness of the shore allowed her to come in very close,
it necessarily promoted heavy breakers, which beat over her with
violence.   On grounding, she broached to, and heeled inwards;
when her mizen-mast soon went over the side, which was shortly

after followed by the others. The people were clinging by the wreck, eagerly expressing their desires to have help; but the spectators, (who had assembled in great numbers,) could not afford any. Unfortunately, she came ashore at the most unpropitious state of the tide, it having just begun to flow, which made her cry and creak a good deal, and she soon began to break up.

It was truly distressing to see so many poor souls surrounded by such imminent danger, and indeed by approaching destruction, and not possessed of any means whereby to assist them, or they possessed of any means to assist themselves; their miserable situation cannot be described. The vessel now breaking up rapidly with the coming tide, there was no alternative, but to tarry on board and perish with her; or to try the event, whether *swimming* and the surf, would assist them to shore. Being reduced to this extreme necessity, the greater part jumped overboard, and engaged in the struggle—it was indeed severe, but short; for the pieces of floating wreck and the surf soon overwhelmed them in one common destruction.

Only two out of all on board came ashore alive, and one of them was floated in upon a ladder. The Horatio being an old vessel, was an entire wreck by nine o'clock. Several of the dead bodies have been thrown ashore much bruised, and cut by the pieces of floating wreck, which no doubt, accelerated their destruction.

JANE and REBECCA, with troops on board, returning from Buenos Ayres, about the beginning of December, 1807, in a dark night and rather squally, very unexpectedly ran upon the rocks under Halziffron Cliff in Mount's Bay, situate about four miles eastward of Helston. As soon as the people on board were sensible of their situation, they fired three or four guns, which alarmed the inhabitants of the neighbourhood, who very soon repaired to the spot. It was so dark, and the cliff towering so much above the vessel, they could not have descryed her, but for the crew having hoisted some lights in the rigging. Notwithstanding the cliff is so difficult of access at any time, several stout hearted

D 2

fellows, from the knowledge they had of the place, and by the
light of their lanthorns, were enabled to go below to assist the
people to land.   On going down they soon discovered a boat
thrown up upon the sand, dry; which they were afterwards given
to understand, had been lowered from the stern of the vessel soon
after she struck, with four men in her, but (in the midst of the
confusion that prevailed) unfortunately without oars; consequently
they could not guide her, so she soon upset, and the men that were
in her perished.   The tide having by this time ebbed pretty much,
the country people were enabled to come very near to the vessel,
and hallooed to them on board to tarry there; for they were afraid
they would be for jumping overboard as they were so close.   The
sailors however in reply, requested them to look out for a buoy
they were going to throw overboard, with a line fast to it.   But,
this expedient was some time before it proved successful, for the
tide favoured its going to sea, and it was carried out into the cove,
and tossed about for some time; when the sailors hauled it on
board again, and sent it in another direction.   At last the people
on shore got hold of it, and by the line hauled the end of a hawser
from over the stern, and several of them by holding on, kept it so
taught as for a sling to run upon it; it was afterwards fastened
to a rock, by which means several men were landed.   But to
make the passage more agreeable and secure for the females, (there
were about ten on board of various ranks, and several children
also,) much time was spent in rigging out a chair; which caused a
great interruption to the debarkation.   The work resumed, and
continued to go on as fast as *their Apparatus* would admit; but
alas! it was too tardy to meet the exigency of the occasion: and
while there were yet a great many on board, about 10 A. M. the
vessel suddenly rent asunder, and precipitated them into the water.
The scene was now awfully distressing, and the heart-rending cries
of the poor perishing creatures, dolefully piercing!

       All that humanity could dictate or courage perform, was
done to render them assistance; but notwithstanding they were
only a very few yards distant, it was not possible to afford preser-

ration only to a very few. Between 40 and 50 perished! As several of the soldiers had a great many dollars in their possession, it was generally believed that the weight of them about their persons, promoted the destruction of many. It was believed also, that the time occupied in contriving for the accommodation of the females, was more than sufficient to have saved all the men.

INVINCIBLE 74 Guns, Capt. Rennie, and having on board Adml. Totty, sailed from Yarmouth 16th March 1801, to join the Baltic fleet; and between two and three o'clock the same afternoon struck on a sandbank. In this situation she continued beating with the greatest violence for near three hours, when the mizen-mast went by the board, and the main-mast was immediately afterwards cut away.—All now gave themselves up for lost.—At this awful moment a fishing smack approached the wreck, on which, two boats belonging to the Invincible were ordered out. On board one of those the admiral, purser, and four midshipmen, and several men reached the fishing smack in safety; as did also the other boat full of people. Both of them immediately returned to the ship, but on again approaching the smack, one was forced away, and every person on board would inevitably have perished, had not a collier, which happened to be passing by at this critical moment, picked them all up. This vessel afterwards afforded every assistance that humanity dictated, or that she was capable of giving, and was the means of saving many of the crew. All the other boats that were attempted to be got overboard were immediately lost.

The fishing smack, with the admiral on board, being unable to afford the least assistance to the ship, remained at anchor during the whole of the night of the 16th. On the approach of day, the master of the vessel expressed an unwilliugness to go near the wreck, but Adml. Totty in direct opposition to him, caused the cable to be cut and proceeded to the ship. Melancholy however to relate, while he was doing every thing of which human exertion is capable, to assist the unhappy people on board, the wreck once more got into deep water and gradually sunk, to the infinite distress

of the admiral. and the other spectators, who were nearly frantic
with grief at this tremendous scene of human misery and destruction.

While the ship was rapidly going down the launch was
heaved out, as many of the crew as she could possibly hold jumped
on board, and had only time to clear the poop, when the vessel,
with 400 souls entirely disappeared, and went to the bottom. A
number of unhappy sufferers attempted to get on board the already
overladen launch, but as no more could be permitted to enter,
without the certain destruction of the whole, they were struck
away with the oars, and in a few seconds were wholly ingulphed
in the pitiless waves. The total number of human beings who
thus found a watery grave was upwards of 400, among whom were
several passengers on their way to join other ships belonging to
the North Sea fleet. All the commissioned officers except two
lieutenants, together with all the officers of marines with most of
their men likewise went to the bottom. About 200 were all that
were saved.

INGEBORD YACHT, in a dark night (1802) pitched on
a sandbank, with her keel almost perpendicularly raised in the air.
The six persons that composed her crew remained some time almost petrified with horror, before they had courage to attempt to
save themselves. In this most dreadful situation they passed seven
hours. They were at length discovered by some fishermen, who
made ready their boat to push out to their relief; but on viewing
their horrid situation, the most courageous turned pale with dread.
Yet moved by compassion, and encouraged by persons present,
they resolved on the dangerous attempt. A long cord was fastened
to the boat and the other end given to those remaining on shore,
to pull back the boat as fast as possible through the breakers, when
they had taken the people from the wreck. Eleven daring men
got into the boat, but were scarcely sailed off, when the sea broke
over her and seemed to swallow them up. But they appeared
again, and by means of their oars, were enabled to reach the
wreck, which they entered by means of ropes that hung down—
at the moment when the boat was on the point of being driven

into the open sea. With immense difficulty they got the four men into the boat, (the other two had already perished.) Too late they gave the signal for return—the boat was seized by the breakers, whirled round, and must infallibly have overset, had the rope indicated a moment later to those on shore, what they were to do.

The boat was now pulled with the rapidity of an arrow through the breakers, and all reached shore in safety.

JOHN and AGNES—from the Courrier, Nov. 21, 1816.—"The John and Agnes, a Leith trader, Tate master, sailed from Newcastle, Friday sennight, and went on shore near Dunbar the following evening, during a tremendous gale.—A young lady and her brother were swept off the deck early on Sunday morning and drowned—and a sailor who attempted to swim ashore also met a watery grave—the mate died in the rigging from cold and fatigue—master, two men and a boy were saved by clinging to the rigging, and two passengers escaped by swimming ashore."

Substance of a letter I received, on the subject, from the Rev. H. Stevenson, to whom I am not personally known,—dated Dunbar.—"The John and Agnes was overtaken with a gale off this coast on the 9th November, and was evidently in danger of being wrecked.—The people on shore on the approach of night were anxious for her fate. About half past nine she came ashore on a flat sandy beach, and as it was very dark no one on shore knew of the accident. By the fortunate escape of a Mr. Bell by swimming ashore from the vessel,—the people of Dunbar were alarmed and immediately the life-boat was put in motion, but to no purpose; for, it was so very dark, the wreck could not be discerned. Anxious as the people on shore were to render assistance to the poor sufferers, they were obliged to wait the approach of day-light, when by means of the life-boat they succeeded in bringing from the wreck those who were remaining alive."

JUNO.—The Brig Jessia, Capt. Williams, has arrived at Dumfries from St. John's.—On the 11th ult. fell in with the wreck of the Juno, Capt. Charles Henry, from New York to Sligo, laden with timber; and found Lorine Charles Dowlie a native of New

York on the wreck, where he had been (on the mast) three days without tasting victuals ; and says 32 (including passengers) perished by the vessel upsetting—having been struck by a heavy sea while laying to. Capt. W. kept by the wreck four hours, before he could attempt to put off his boat, it blowing a gale of wind, with a high sea, during which time the poor man was making all the signals in his power with his hat.

JOHN, Carson Master, of Garliestown, was lost 26th January, 1817, off the Isle of Man. The master and a boy drowned.

KITTY, from Belfast to Liverpool, was totally lost 27th December, 1816, on Hoyle Bank; all on board perished !

LORD MELVILLE, with 400 troops on board, was lost in Court Mashery Bay, Ireland, Jan. 1816. She drove among the rocks, and the situation of the people on board being very alarming, a boat was very soon launched, and manned with five sailors; two officers, two ladies, a surgeon, a sergeant with his wife and child, also got into her. She had proceeded but a very little way when she was swamped, and only one of the seamen was saved. Fortunately the vessel was a strong one, and the tide also ebbing, favoured her keeping together; and at low water, under Providence, all the rest of the people were enabled to get safe to land.

LITCHFIELD, 50 Guns, wrecked upon the coast of Africa, November, 1758. Says Lieut. Sunderland, "At six in the morning of the 29th November, I was awaked by a great shock; and a confused noise of the men on deck. I ran up, thinking some ship had run foul of us; for by my own reckoning, and that of every other person in the ship, we were at least 35 leagues distant from land—but before I could reach the quarter deck, the ship gave a great stroke upon the ground, and the sea broke all over her; just after this I could perceive the land, rocky, rugged, and uneven, about two cables' length from us. The ship laying with her broadside to windward, the masts soon went overboard, carrying some men with them. It is impossible for any but a sufferer to feel our distress at this time, the masts, yards, and sails, laying alongside in a confused heap, the ship beating violently upon the rocks, the waves curling up to an incredible height, then dashing down with such force, as if they would immediately have split the ship to pieces, which we indeed every moment expected. When we had a little recovered from our first confusion, we saw it necessary to get every thing we could over the larboard side, to prevent the ship from heeling off, and exposing the deck to the sea. Some of the people were very earnest to get the boats out; contrary to advice, and after much entreaty, notwithstanding a most terrible sea, one of the boats was launched, and eight of the best men jumped into it, but it had hardly got to the ship's stern when it was whirled to the bottom and every soul in it perished! The rest of the boats were soon washed to pieces upon deck. We then made a raft with the davit capstan bars and some boards, and waited with resignation for Divine Providence to assist us. The ship was soon filled with water, so we had no time to get up any provisions; the quarter deck and poop were now the only places we could stand on with any security, the waves being mostly spent by the time they reached us, owing to the forepart of the ship breaking them.

At four o'clock in the afternoon, perceiving the sea to be much abated, one of our people attempted to swim, and got safe on shore. There were a number of Moors upon the rock ready to take hold of any one, and beckoned much for us to come ashore, which at first we took for kindness; but they soon undeceived us for they had not the humanity to assist any body that was entirely naked, but would fly to those who had any thing about them, and strip them before they were quite out of the water; in the mean time the poor wretches were left to crawl up the rocks, if they were able, if not, they perished unregarded. The second lieutenant and myself, with about 65 others got ashore before dark.

November 30, at six in the morning, we went down with a number of our men upon the rocks to assist our shipmates in coming ashore, and found the ship had been greatly shattered in the

E

night. It being now low water many attempted to swim ashore;
some got safe, but others perished. The people on board got the
raft into the water, and about 15 men placed themselves upon it.
They had no sooner put off from the wreck, than it overturned;
most of the men recovered it again, but, scarcely were they on,
before it was a second time overturned. Only three or four got
hold of it again, and all the rest perished!—In the mean time, a
good swimmer brought with much difficulty, a rope ashore, which
I had the good fortune to catch hold, just when he was quite spent,
and had thoughts of quitting it. Some people coming to my assistance, we pulled a large rope ashore with that, and made it fast
round a rock. We found this gave great spirits to the poor souls
upon the wreck: for, it being hauled taught from the upper part
of the stern, made an easy descent to any who had art enough to
walk or slide upon a rope, with a smaller rope fixed above to hold
by. This was a means of saving a number of lives, though *many
were washed off* by the impetuous surf and perished. The flood
coming on, raised the surf, and prevented any more from coming
at that time, so that the ropes could be of no farther use. We
then retired from the rocks: and hunger prevailing we broiled
some of the turkeys, &c.—which made our first meal upon this
barbarous coast. The surf greatly increasing with the flood, and
breaking upon the forepart of the ship, she was divided into three
parts; the forepart was turned keel up; the middle part was
dashed into a thousand pieces; the forepart of the poop fell also
at this time, and about 30 of the people went with it, eight of
whom got ashore with our help, but so bruised that we despaired
of their recovery. Nothing but the afterpart of the poop now
remained above water, with a very small part of the other decks,
on which our captain, and about 130 more remained, expecting
every wave to be their last. Every shock threw some off; few or
none of whom came ashore alive. During this distress, the Moors
laughed uncommonly, and seemed much diverted when a wave
larger than usual threatened the destruction of the poor tottering
souls upon the wreck.—Between four and five o'clock the sea was

much decreased with the ebb : the rope being still secure, the people began to venture upon it; some tumbled off and perished; others got safe ashore. About five we beckoned as much as possible for the captain to come upon the rope, as this seemed to be as good an opportunity as we had seen, and many had come safe with our assistance ; and just before it was dark, we saw him come upon the rope, he was closely followed by a good able seaman, who did all he could to keep up his spirits and to assist him in warping. As he could not swim and had been so many hours without refreshment, with the surf hurling him violently along, he was no longer able to resist the violence of the waves, and had lost his hold of the great rope, and must inevitably have perished, had not a wave thrown him within reach of our ropes, which he had barely sufficient sense left to catch hold of. We pulled him up, and after resting a short time on the rocks, he came to himself and walked up to the tent, desiring us still to assist the people in coming ashore. The Moors would have stripped him, though he had nothing on but a plain waistcoat and breeches, if we had not plucked up a little spirit and opposed them.

The people continued to come ashore, though many perished in the attempt :—we had firebrands also, to let the poor men upon the wreck see we were still there ready to assist them.—About nine at night, finding no more men venture upon the rope, as the surf was again greatly increased, we retired to the tent, leaving between 30 and 40 persons upon the wreck.

December 1, in the morning the weather was moderate and fair ; but we found the wreck all in pieces upon the rocks, and the shore covered with lumber. In the afternoon we called a muster and found our number to be 220, so that 130 must have been drowned.

LEONORA—a French vessel, lost 16th April, 1817.

"ENGLISH HEROISM."—The following is taken from the Evening Courier of April 24th :—translated from the Moniteur— Calais, April 17th. " Yesterday the wind blowing from N. N. E. with extreme violence, had rendered the sea frightful and all

approach to the coast dangerous, when about eleven o'clock A. M.
the time of high water, there was seen a small French vessel
(which is since known to be the Leonora, from L'Orient, of
72 tons, with seven men, bound from Nantes to Dunkirk, with
a cargo of grain) beating up painfully against the fury of the
waves.

The captain (Huard) thinking no doubt, that it would be
safer to attempt entering the port of Calais than laying out to sea,
determined on the former; and although he had neither a pilot on
board, nor any personal knowledge of the coast, he hazarded an
effort to carry it into execution; but overpowered by the force of
the wind, the current, and the waves, he was driven on the works
to the east of the port, where he stuck.

The danger now became imminent, and the wrecks thrown
ashore, announced the certain destruction of the seven unfortunate
mariners. Numerous witnesses of the scene of desolation lamented
that they could offer no assistance. At this moment there was seen
a pinnace boat advancing with force of oars, sent from the British
Yacht, Royal Sovereign, which had carried to this port the Duke
of Orleans a few days ago. This boat commanded by Lieut.
Charles Moore, who had under him eight sailors from the crew of
the Yacht, advanced with intrepidity in spite of the dangers with
which it was surrounded. Capt. Owen the commander of the
Yacht, displaying a zeal worthy of the greatest praise, stood upon
the extremity of the pier, and cheered by his gestures and his voice,
the brave lieutenant and his eight sailors. And although he was
incessantly covered with the waves that dashed against the pier, he
perseveringly maintained his painful and dangerous situation, for
the purpose of pointing out, together with Mr. Sagot the port
captain, and some other French officers, the measures proper to
be adopted, and of adding if possible to the necessary means of
assistance. Up to this time the danger had been increasing on
board the wrecked vessel, and already had several men lost their
lives, when there were some seen still to survive and to implore
assistance. Meanwhile the generous and intrepid lieutenant and his

eight sailors neglected no effort. At last they reached within a little distance of the wreck, and by means of a rope which they threw out to the vessel, saved two of these unfortunate men. Not being able any longer to keep their position, the boat returned to the pier to land these two, when Capt. Wilkinson of the English Packet Dart, of Dover, generously threw himself into the boat, at the hazard of his life to assist in this manoeuvre. There remained still on the wreck another survivor who had bound himself to the mast with a rope that he might not be washed overboard. The desire of crowning this fine action by rescuing another victim from the waves, inspired regrets into the courageous lieut. and his crew. They returned anew to face a danger, the force of which they had already measured, and had nearly reached the wreck, the gallant lieutenant standing up and directing the rowers, when a wave more impetuous than the rest, broke over the pinnace and precipitated this generous officer into the water, who instantly disappeared. A feeling of consternation, struck with terror and regret the numerous spectators of the scene. The lieutenant however after having passed under his boat, recovered himself and rose to the surface, when he was immediately taken up by the sailors, and replaced in the boat. The courage of this generous man was not slackened by the threatened death which he had so miraculously escaped. He lost not the presence of mind that belongs to true intrepidity, and he returned with perseverance towards the perishing individual, for whose safety he hazarded his own. The difficulty of the situation increased: the French sailor, too much weakened had lost courage, but seeing the boat return to his assistance, he unbound himself, and endeavouring to make an effort for his own salvation, he precipitated himself into the sea, where he was seen to float for an instant, and then to sink for ever. All assistance had now become useless, the English boat returned to port, where the generous men who had given so noble an example of rare intrepidity, received the testimonies of that satisfaction with which every spectator was so deeply penetrated."

MARIA, Capt. Clarke, lost in the gale of September 3d, 1816, on Happlesburgh Rock, and all on board perished!

' MINSTRELL, Rosignal, from Alicant to Jersey, totally lost with all her crew off Roscoff.

NOORDSTAR, Weesenburg, from Amsterdam to Dunkirk, was totally lost on the Long Sand, on Friday evening the 4th April, 1817. The master, mate, one seaman and one boy drowned.

O'DONNEL, from Galway to Belfast, was lost with all her crew off Blackhead.—April, 1817.

PHÆNIX, 44 Guns, Capt. Sir Hyde Parker, lost in 1780 on the coast of Cuba. Two men got ashore with a line, and by this means got a hawser and made it fast to the rocks; upon which many ventured, and arrived safe ashore. There were some sick and wounded on board who could not avail themselves of this method. Some died of the wounds they received in getting ashore.

PHÆTON, American Brig of 200 Tons, from Cayenne to Gottenburgh, having on board Jean Jacques Aymé and other passengers. The vessel had encountered severe weather for some weeks, and was now got upon the coast of Scotland, with which those on board were not acquainted.—They were near to Fraserburgh, but they thought it had been Montrose. The captain ordered several guns to be fired, and hoisted a signal to call on board a coasting pilot, but no one appearing and night coming on he stood into a bay;—they were not a quarter of a league from land, in five fathoms water, and let go an anchor in hopes of being able to enter the harbour in the morning. In the mean time, the sea continued to be boisterous and the vessel was tossed about almost as much as before. About two o'clock in the morning the captain ordered a second anchor to be let go. The sea now struck the vessel with so much violence, that the water broke in abundance upon the deck, and frequently found its way down the scuttle, between decks. This accident at first took place only every quarter of an hour; but, about four o'clock, it became so frequent, that the captain apprehensive of foundering ordered the

cables to be cut, approached within musket shot of the coast and
dropped the sheet anchor, the only one that they had left. This
manoeuvre did not much better their fate. The waves were as
frequent, and became so violent that about seven o'clock the cable
parted and they were driven ashore. She struck repeatedly, and
at every stroke, they thought that the vessel would go to pieces.
This fortunately did not happen; if it had, though they were very
near the land, not one of them could have escaped; but the vessel
having opened in several places, and the water rushing in on all
sides, they were obliged to go upon deck, whence they discovered,
at 50 yards from them, as the day appeared, the inhabitants of
Fraserburgh, who seemed very much concerned at their perilous
situation, but none of them durst attempt to come to their assistance; it was impossible indeed, to cross this space, full of rocks,
against which the sea was breaking with the greatest violence: not
one of the sailors had the courage to expose himself to its fury.—
About ten o'clock, an attempt was made to get out the longboat,
but she immediately filled: the men who were benumbed with
cold, tried in vain to bale her out; they were under the necessity
of quitting her, and by the impulse of the sea, having been thrown
upon the rocks which lined the coast, she was dashed to pieces
against them.

The waves which had been continually striking the vessel
on the starboard side, now imperceptibly heeled her, and obliged
the crew to take refuge on the higher side, that they might not be
entirely under water. About noon some heavy waves laid the
vessel down on her beam ends, so that the main-mast was in a
horizontal position above the water, and might have served as a
brow to get near the shore, had it not been continually covered by
the waves; their situation was now become very frightful.

The sailors, who could speak English, did not cease to
implore the assistance of the numerous spectators on shore;—but,
alas! it was not in their power to afford them the required aid.
Twenty men were seen on the beach carrying on their backs a
boat, which they had fetched from the harbour, at more than a

mile distance. The sight of this gave the unfortunate sufferers some hope. In the mean time Ayme felt himself quite exhausted, &c. &c. On looking round he saw several of his ship-mates floating corpses.

About three o'clock, amidst the approaching signs of death, and at a time when he neither expected nor wished for assistance, he perceived on the beach a young man naked, who plunged into the sea, which was now become somewhat smoother. In a little time he was in the midst of the sufferers, having swam off with a rope fastened to that boat which had been recently brought by the twenty men. The sailors by means of this rope hauled on board the boat, in which several persons were put. Another rope fixed to the shore, served to draw back the boat in a diagonal direction, and to prevent her from driving on the rocks, which were opposite the vessel. This boat having made a second trip, Ayme was then put into her. He had not strength sufficient to quit his place: two sailors took him from it, and put him into the boat half dead. He was brought on shore senseless; but by very great exertions at an Inn to which he was carried and put to bed, he was at length restored to life. The American captain was brought safely to shore, but he died in consequence of the great fatigue he had endured. Several of the crew and passengers perished on board the wreck.

PEGGY, of Bamf, West Master, from Leith to Bamf with salt and staves, was lost to the south of Aberdeen,—all hands unfortunately perished.—November, 1816.

RANGER.—This ship was lost in the gale of the 1st September, 1816, near Munsley,—all the crew perished except the carpenter.

REPULSE of 64 Guns, lost on the coast of France, March 1800. After detailing the wreck, the writer says,—" I forgot to mention that while the boats were employed in landing the people, those on board had thrown the ends of several hawsers on shore which the peasantry made fast to the rocks, and which being hauled taught on board, they could go upon them with great ease.

Two men however being intoxicated, fell off the hawsers into the water and perished—and four marines lay on deck dead drunk, (and who I believe were not carried ashore) must have perished also!".

RESOLUTION, of London, from Oporto (laden with near 400 pipes of wine, 200 boxes of oranges, &c.) on Saturday the 4th of January, 1817, got embayed in Mount's Bay and came to an anchor off Porthleaven. After riding for some time in a very heavy sea, she parted her cable. She soon let go another anchor, and brought up; but at the approach of night and also of the flood tide, her situation was viewed with much anxiety by many people assembled upon the shore. To draw the attention of the poor sailors, lighted candles were placed in the window of a public house, situated on the top of the cliff just over that part of the beach, which was most favourable for them to run their vessel upon, in case coming ashore was unavoidable. As the cable they had parted was their best, the captain was doubtful of the remaining one holding out the night; and the breakers being very heavy upon the shore, it was concluded that their lives would be placed in a most perilous situation, if they should be forced ashore upon a flowing tide. It was therefore deemed adviseable for their preservation, to cut their cable and run in just upon the top of the tide, or at the beginning of the ebb. This was done, and by the assistance of the signals from the shore, the vessel was run in upon the very spot that afforded the best ground and the smoothest water in the whole bay. But notwithstanding these favourables, the situation of the crew was hazardous, as the sea beat over the vessel with great violence, and threatened destruction; the fear of which the poor fellows did not fail to express, but which to avoid, (by being washed overboard,) they took to the rigging, and very prudently made no attempt to escape, until the receding of the water afforded the fishermen the opportunity of throwing the end of a line to them; by which they drew a rope on board, and by it were all safely conveyed to land.

F

SAPOR, Stetson, from New York to London, was totally
lost with *all her crew*, on the Island of Sark.—Feb. 15, 1817.

SAMUEL, Harman, from Charante to London, lost 4th
March on the Island of Oleron, master and one man drowned.

SPECULATOR, Ratton, from Cette to Rotterdam, lost on
Goree Island, 10th March, master and part of the crew drowned.

SCEPTRE, 64 Guns, was at anchor (with several other
ships of war) in Table Bay, 5th November 1799, when it came on
to blow a heavy gale from N. W. the wind in that quarter blows direct into the bay—a little after noon she parted her cable ; the sheet
anchor was immediately let go, and the sheet cable veered away
to twenty-eight fathoms. The gale still continued to increase in
fury : at two o'clock the vessel parted from her best bower cable,
the crew immediately let go the spare anchor, but in veering it
away they slipped the spare cable, the end of it not being secured.
The launch was now hoisted out, to endeavour to get the end of
a cable from his Majesty's ship Jupiter. She was, however, unfortunately upset, and totally lost together with the crew. From
two till half past six minute guns of distress were fired, and the
ensign hoisted Union downwards. At seven when the ship parted
from her sheet anchor, the utmost confusion prevailed on board,
from a too precipitate order *for every man to provide for his own
safety*. She continued to drive at the mercy of the waves for about
ten minutes, when she struck on a reef of rocks, broadside to the
shore, heeling on her larboard side towards the sea. The captain
now ordered the main and mizen masts to be cut away, and soon
after the fore-mast went by the board.—Despairing of assistance
from the shore, several of the crew now leaped overboard ; but
from the eddy caused by the wreck, they were carried out to sea,
in spite of the aid which those on board endeavoured to afford
them.

About half past nine o'clock the poop was washed away,
and seventy or eighty of the crew jumping overboard, reached it
with much difficulty. They had nearly gained the shore, when a

heavy sea striking the afterpart, it went end for end over, and
every person upon it perished. The wreck soon afterwards heeled
in towards the shore, and upon heeling off again, it rent fore and
aft, parting in two places.—No language can describe the horrors
of that fatal moment.—A horrid yell was heard for about a minute, after which all was silent; the wreck having instantly dashed
to pieces most of the unfortunate sufferers. It was at this time that
the captain, the officers, and a great part of the crew, lost their
lives. The only officers saved from the wreck, were Mr. Shaw,
master's mate, and Messrs. Spink and Buddle, midshipmen; together with about forty-seven seamen and one marine. Out of
these, nine died of their wounds on the beach.—Had it not been
for the assistance afforded by the light dragoons, who rode into the
surf, it is more than probable that every soul would have perished.
Three waggon loads of dead were next morning taken to a place
near the hospital, and there interred. About 100 more bodies,
miserably mangled, were buried in one hole on the beach.

The Sceptre had on board many of the trophies taken at
Seringapatam, which were consequently lost with the ship.

SAN JUAN PRINCIPE, Frigate. The feelings of admiration will be powerfully excited by a perusal of the subjoined
letter, which was written from Gibraltar, by Mr. Alexander Wilson,
son of Mr. Wilson, watchmaker in Kelso: and, while admiring
the heroism which he displayed in the melancholy circumstances
which called it forth, the reader will be pleased with the simplicity
and modesty which characterize the narrative.

Gibraltar, April 19, 1807.—"On Sunday the 5th Instant, I
witnessed a scene of horror I can never forget:—a Portuguese
Frigate, the San Juan Principe, Capt. R. I. F. Lobo, was re-
ported to be wrecked on the east coast, about four miles from the
Spanish Lines. About eight o'clock in the morning, I could
plainly perceive with a glass, the vessel dismasted, and a great
number of men on board. A friend of mine, Mr. Masser, and I,
immediately took horse and arrived on the beach about nine.

We found that the ship had at that moment almost gone to pieces, and about 200 men were floating on the fragments of the wreck, and driving towards the mouth of a small river, which was swelled by the late rains. At the same time a tremendous sea set in, which had raised a bank of sand at its mouth. A number of Spaniards were looking on. I instantly plunged into the river, and found I could ford it about shoulder deep. Mr. Masser followed me, and four or five Spaniards imitated our example. For two hours we were employed in snatching from a watery grave the unfortunate creatures, who were clinging to pieces of timber, and dashing every moment upon the bank of sand, and upon each other. I with difficulty saved Capt. Lobo; he was driving upon a piece of the vessel, almost exhausted, and senseless—the next breaker in all probability, would have been his end.—I dragged up the second captain; and shortly after a lieutenant, who expired on my landing him on the beach: I likewise saved a midshipman; as did Mr. Masser, the purser: these are all the officers saved. The crew consisted of 315, out of which there are 116 survivors. I pledge you my word, more than two-thirds of that number owe their lives to Mr. Masser's exertions and my own. One officer and four men died in my arms, from being bruised and exhausted before I could land them. Many a poor fellow we were obliged to let go, from the quantity of wood driving in every direction, and saw them dashed to pieces on the sand. The sight was most dreadful, but the cause we were embarked in nerved our arms. About half past twelve, nine of the unhappy sufferers remained upon the last piece of the wreck. Many of the garrison arrived about this time, and with their assistance, four of them were got ashore. Mr. Masser and myself had many hair-breadth escapes; he was, at one time, swept from his feet by a breaker; I was most fortunately near, and, making a dash, caught hold of his coat as he was floating in the surge, and by the assistance of one of the Spaniards saved him and a sailor. I was, as you may suppose, very poorly for some time, from the bruises and over-exertion; but I am now recovered.

God grant that I may never witness so melancholy a sight again; but should that be my fate, God grant that I may have it in my power to be equally serviceable to...

SWEDISH GALLIOT, from Gergento, lost off Port Mahon—only four sailors saved.—March 1817.

SEAHORSE TRANSPORT, wrecked 30th January 1816, in Tramore Bay, near Waterford, Ireland. She dragged while riding at two anchors, and in about an hour after she grounded, went to pieces.—This was a most melancholy wreck—twenty-eight only were saved out of 394 men, women, and children, who were on board.

TWO FRIENDS TRANSPORT, sailed from Portsmouth, 1805, with part of the 100th Regt.—October 22d at night, going eight knots an hour, ran upon the rocks—being high water beat over the outer rocks into two fathoms water. As day-light approached, an attempt was made to hoist out the jolly-boat, but it was hardly raised when a heavy sea sent it in pieces among the rocks. About ten A. M. our hopes began to revive a little, by the appearance of a man making towards the shore. From him we learned that we were on the Island of Cape Breton, about a mile and half from the ruins of Louisburgh. Having acquainted him with our distress, he went away, and in some hours afterwards, brought a very small boat to our assistance. As the boat could not contain above four persons, and the surf continued still very high, only one half of our people could be landed this day. Night was now fast coming on, and every one solicitous to get ashore. A young officer of the 41st Regt. and myself formed the resolution of getting ashore by a rope that was attached to the vessel; he accordingly commenced his attempt, but losing his hold, was dashed among the rocks, and in about two hours afterwards, was found a lifeless mangled corpse upon the beach. The untimely fate of this amiable young gentleman appalled my courage, and prevented me from running such a risk. The unfortunate issue of the undertaking was not, however, sufficient to deter others from making the attempt; and two privates fell victims to the fury of the waves. It was now dark, and no more people could be landed from the wreck; nothing therefore could be done till the morning, and never I believe, did any set of mortals pass a more melancholy night than we did. The morning at last began to dawn, and by renewed efforts, the officers, with nearly all the people were safe ashore. I continued animating and encouraging the remaining few left on board, &c.

TROIS AMIS, of Bordeaux, bound to Rouen, was totally lost near Bridport, during the gale of Sunday night (Jan. 19th, 1817) only one passenger saved.

Courier, 29th November, 1816. A vessel laden with hemp was totally lost at Faroe's Head, near Loch Eribol, on the night of 15th inst. during a gale from N. N. W. and all hands perished.

FINIS.

Paddon, Printer, Penryn.

Lightning Source UK Ltd.
Milton Keynes UK
UKHW020750170420
361818UK00003B/82